## Introduction

Hello, and welcome to the book that's going to show you ways on how to discover who you truly are, and achieve greater heights of accomplishments in your life. In other words, during and after reading this book you're find greatness within the way you perceive things from now on.

What you know and do is the outcome of what should be.

This book will show you things you haven't considered before now, and it's also going to give you insights that can and will change the way you see and do things as well.

You will have epiphanies and "ah ha" moments throughout its reading; so be prepared to become a different (no better) person from this point forward. You will find yourself being more aware than what you've imagined being. A very bright-light will come-on inside your comprehensions to better living conditions, so be ready to see things in a whole new light.

It's your life, so let the visions in this book show you how to become the person you were meant to be, living the life you were meant to live. And be ready to see your life taking better form from what's about to take place inside your lifestyle.

This book is going to awaken you, and keep you aware of the many wonderful things going-on in and around you every day.

You will learn how to come in contact with your inner-strengths!

Open this Door; and discover Real Living!


So, shall we begin?

Wisdom and Understanding

Inner-Contents

## The Hidden Power Within You

Are you aware of your inner-power, and how to have control of it?

Before getting into the many visions within this amazing book; let's do something you may-have not considered doing before now. It's called "Tapping into your inner source of power." You have the power to pull people and things to your life, or push them away with just a simple awareness of being able to do it.

(You can do more with your life, if you awaken to the power within your own existence!)

For instance... Take a piece of thin-thread about twelve inches long and tie it to a paper-clip, or a simple ring. Now, hold the tip of the thread between your index finger and thumb, then rest your elbow on a flat-surface; (lift your hand-up with the object on the string hanging freely.) – It's called a Pendulum.

(Look at the object and give it a command to go around in circles in either direction, or back-and-forth with a Yes, No, or Maybe answer to each movement.)

Make sure the object on the string is still, and not moving... Then mentally tell the object to move back-and-forth, or in a circle, left or right. – Give it a second, but concentrate on the object on the string; then it will move the way you command it to.

– (You have now come in contact with your inner will-power, and also have control of it!)

Test your Pendulum!... Right now, ask your Pendulum to answer a question. And watch it move according to a "Yes" or "No" answer; or even a "Maybe" movement sign.

This is only showing you the power you possess inside you. – You're seeing how to be in touch with your own inner-strength, nothing more.

Do you realize, you are already using this same energy to create the lifestyle you are living right now; and without your awareness of it? You should know that this powerful technique is at your disposal whenever you choose; so start enhancing your awareness of knowing you have the power to create the lifestyle you truly want.

Put this awareness to use and start creating the occurrences you want to see taking place in your life! But remember this, it's only making you more aware of your own inner-abilities to create a more productive and effective lifestyle so you'll be driven to learn more about the way you live each day, nothing more – unless you make it more than what's being shown to you. But that's entirely up to you.

A word of caution:

I highly recommend, that you don't use this Pendulum to measure your entire life with it, because in reality, you are the Pendulum with all the decisions you make each day, and this book is going to show you that you truly are. – Your decisions for your success is based on your inner-awareness and how much you believe in yourself; not some object!

## The Hidden Power Within You

Are you aware of your inner-power, and how to have control of it?

Before getting into the many visions within this amazing book; let's do something you may-have not considered doing before now. It's called "Tapping into your inner source of power." You have the power to pull people and things to your life, or push them away with just a simple awareness of being able to do it.

(You can do more with your life, if you awaken to the power within your own existence!)

For instance... Take a piece of thin-thread about twelve inches long and tie it to a paper-clip, or a simple ring. Now, hold the tip of the thread between your index finger and thumb, then rest your elbow on a flat-surface; (lift your hand-up with the object on the string hanging freely.) – It's called a Pendulum.

(Look at the object and give it a command to go around in circles in either direction, or back-and-forth with a Yes, No, or Maybe answer to each movement.)

Make sure the object on the string is still, and not moving... Then mentally tell the object to move back-and-forth, or in a circle, left or right. – Give it a second, but concentrate on the object on the string; then it will move the way you command it to.

– (You have now come in contact with your inner will-power, and also have control of it!)

Test your Pendulum!... Right now, ask your Pendulum to answer a question. And watch it move according to a "Yes" or "No" answer; or even a "Maybe" movement sign.

This is only showing you the power you possess inside you. – You're seeing how to be in touch with your own inner-strength, nothing more.

Do you realize, you are already using this same energy to create the lifestyle you are living right now; and without your awareness of it? You should know that this powerful technique is at your disposal whenever you choose; so start enhancing your awareness of knowing you have the power to create the lifestyle you truly want.

Put this awareness to use and start creating the occurrences you want to see taking place in your life! But remember this, it's only making you more aware of your own inner-abilities to create a more productive and effective lifestyle so you'll be driven to learn more about the way you live each day, nothing more – unless you make it more than what's being shown to you. But that's entirely up to you.

A word of caution:

I highly recommend, that you don't use this Pendulum to measure your entire life with it, because in reality, you are the Pendulum with all the decisions you make each day, and this book is going to show you that you truly are. – Your decisions for your success is based on your inner-awareness and how much you believe in yourself; not some object!

The Pendulum is not 100% accurate. Well, not in the beginning of using it. – It will probably take many years to master this practice, because you will have to give it a lot of your inner-awareness to achieve this accomplishment!

And there's no greater achievement than being able to harness your own inner-power and using it at your own discretion. Only use the Pendulum to see your inner-strengths.

This book is going to show you that you are a Pendulum, and how to remove doubts, regrets, lies, trickeries, or any other illusions that kept you from living the life you were meant to live. – You are the commander of your life; and these visions will help you see how, when, where, and why you are the only one making things happen in your life every day – no one else!

Life is designed for you to have choices, not challenges. But some people prefer to see it that way. – (But you be the judge of it!)

As you read throughout this book, you'll notice your comprehensions receiving the same energy-source you get from the Pendulum.

You will feel yourself growing wiser and becoming more understandable with each page of enlightenments; it's going to give you more to make your life more enjoyable.

While reading this book, stay aware of this energy you discovered with the Pendulum. It's going to help enlighten your understandings further into a world of more possibilities.

And after you finish reading this book the first time, start re-reading it again. – But this time, read it slower and let all visions absorb deep inside your awareness to be part of transforming your life into better living conditions and create the lifestyle you want to live.

Let these visions assist you making yourself into a better person, living better than you've ever imagined. Then the life you want will start happening naturally for you every day, everywhere you are.

Allow your comprehensions to come-out of looking only in one direction. Let your awareness move in different angles, having a different outlook on things from now on; and you'll have a better perspective concerning your life, to see what true living really is!

Now, let's begin ...

# Wisdom and Understanding

## Am I Applying It To My Life

Before getting into knowing if you are applying wisdom and understanding to your life; this book will show many ways of how to express it, explain it, translate it, instruct others with it, and correct yourself. You'll be wiser and more understandable when you're done reading this book.

Wisdom means the ability to discern or judge what's true, right, or lasting; insight. – And understanding means a wise outlook, plan, or course of action. Other definitions will be applied while reading this book.

The main topic is you having an awareness of what true wisdom and understanding is first; then seeing how to apply it on a higher plane of reality concerning everything else in life. And this book wasn't written to coach you into viewing monetary values. Well, not indirectly, even though you will hear simple instructions on how to create "more money" through the slip-streams of your comprehensions at any given moment.

Most information you hear, captures you from desiring something out of desperation. – In other words, through your needing state of mind.

The governing system knows everyone desire more of what they have, or don't have. They control society with this awareness, which isn't always a bad thing. Even though it does control a large portion of society's way of communicating successfully. And yet, it protects society at the same time.

We mainly buy Information – but true Wisdom and true Understanding comes to all those seeking it. – All you have to do is truly want it, and it shall be given. That's why you should read this book throughout its entirety.

Remember, this! There's a generation coming that's going to take a book like this and turn the world around toward its intended course to real living, by making Wisdom and Understanding the most amazing discovery humankind has ever known.

Let me say something before we begin: An "Add to Cart" switch wasn't intended for this book; but it will provide monetary support to help build an adult GED housing and training facility for those living without a high-school equivalence, (mainly the homeless); and for future publication funding.

Homelessness (how to help stop it) is the main target for financial support.

See website for more details www.missionimprovement1.com

Wisdom and Understanding will Crown anyone's head if they carry-out their messages freely to the whole layout of humankind. And the reason why most people struggle or suffer so greatly in many areas of their lives, is they haven't realized we must be wiser if we're going to express love and happiness on a higher scale concerning humankind.

The problem with drawing more people closer; is not being open enough to appreciate those natural encounters and natural desires we have for each other.

If you open your mind and see wisdom and understanding like a huge water-fall flowing down inside your thoughts and visions, you will instantly change and feel refreshments to a whole new world of seeing how to become a better you.

You see, wisdom and understanding shows you the process of giving, not just having. And true wealth isn't measured by how much you have, it's measured by how much you can give. Because when you want something just to have it; it becomes another form of being had. It's not entirely yours to have alone. Mainly, you're only using it for a short period of time – that makes you feel more like you only had something. And selfishness can be the result of just having something for yourself. – But when it's gone, that makes you feel like you've been, had.

When you are enlightened with the desire to have "more" to give, you'll feel everything flowing to you naturally (whether you keep it or not.) And it makes you feel like you are doing more with your life. – You'll feel like you're being more than what you are.

When you're in this mode of thinking, you'll have the attention of everyone around you. Because the law of gravity moves with the slightest hint of any pulling sensation. Inside these pages you'll feel the gravitational pulling sensation that exists inside you, life, and everyone else around you, naturally.

Your thoughts and ideas will improve while absorbing the many visions these pages will provide you. You'll naturally feel them reshaping your mind and your lifestyle.

And if you are not feeling these visions coming inside your awareness, then you are denying them like putting-up an umbrella blocking them. The umbrella is your denial of true wisdom and understanding.

Do you enjoy worldly information more than true wisdom and understanding?

Well... Do you? If you do, then you are denying the very essence of your own existence.

Now, feel this water-fall of true Wisdom and Understanding coming inside your entire awareness instead of upon your mind, because you are opening-up to it; and it will fill your comprehensions with non-stop rewards to greater achievements from this point forward, every minute of each day.

And you will feel the difference.

The way success works, is when you let life come inside you, instead upon you. In other words, let life impregnate you with the expectations of its natural causes like everything else does. It doesn't matter if you are male or female; you must be impregnated and endure the birth-pains of any desire you have out of life.

There are tons of natural causes each of us must endure during the entire course of our lifetime; causes such as, loving others, being happy, successful living, untold amount of funding projects, relationships of all kinds; (Use your imagination.)

Now...What are the birth-pains?

Anytime you're having an experience with discomforts; that's the birth-pains of it. And anytime you're not getting along with someone in a relationship, it's the birth-pains of dealing with that person, or vice versa. You're allowing that person to be in your lifestyle and it hurts sometimes when you're making room for them.

Being upset, angry, disappointed, frustrated, unhappy, or feeling hurt by someone, are the birth-pains in any relationship. You're dealing with a different person's behaviors.

If you want a relationship with anyone; (deal with the birth-pains that comes with them!)

If you look closer at life, you'll see exactly how this is happening. And a lot of what you're doing is like being in a position of a woman giving birth to a child. But some people treat life like a miscarriage; miscarrying most of everything they say, or do.

So when someone comes into your life, treat them like you just allowed them to interject their lifestyle inside yours. See that person as though you are a life giving experience to them. And if you start a new relationship with someone then change your mind; you have basically caused an abortion because of abandoning the opportunity they're giving you to carry.

Society calls it a change of mind, or a change of heart. – No. It's a miscarriage, or an abortion of (someone new) trying to be born in your lifestyle – nothing less.

When you are really prosperous; you'll feel everything like it's being injected inside your lifestyle – an in or out performance is occurring in any situation. Give and take is what some of us call it. – It's the same way seeing humankind being created. Sowing seeds in the ground. Putting a plan of action in place. Sticking an electrical plug inside a wall-socket, placing batteries inside something, or sticking a gas nozzle inside a car.

– There are so many examples for seeing this activity going-on everywhere. (Use your imagination.)

As long as you are aware of this; no challenge will ever overcome your truest power of attracting. An in and out occurrence is always taking place in every situation of life.

That's why you are always going in and out of relationships with other people. – Apply these insights and never miscarry or abandon another relationship with anyone else, ever again.

This book is naturally injecting newer visions inside your awareness. You are being impregnated with newer understandings by discovering more thoughts and answers to becoming a more attractive you.

If you feel like you're standing-still inside your comprehensions while reading this book; then don't worry, it's just the nature of these visions helping you see a better you.

And if you've been living backward instead of moving forward; then this book is going to show you how to turn your life around putting you on the course you intended.

Now what does it mean, by living backwards?

If you spend most of your time thinking about past situations, remembering what you did and said, doing the same things repeatedly every day, each week, monthly, and year round – then wakeup, and realize you're going through life thinking, talking, and acting backwards when you should be seeing, hearing, and feeling yourself moving forward.

Another thing to remember (if this is the case.) For those of you holding your head down while walking – stop looking like a victim of circumstance! You are projecting an image of someone walking with a broken spirit. Don't walk looking down on life as though you have regrets – raise your head and look forward to the things that are yet to come.

**Don't look down on life, raise your head and spirit, and look forward to it!**

Raise your spirit, and acknowledge a life of giving, not regretting. Don't spend any more time trying to reach the finish line to anything else; just enjoy the race!

Be still inside, and allow things to happen naturally, because you want things to change in your favor. Allow these (brilliant visions) to come inside you awareness, naturally.

Just keep up with the things you do – or you'll find yourself trying to catch-up to them!

Everything you think-of, and do from-now-on, these visions will assist you. – You'll be more successful, whether you believe it or not!

No matter what others think about you – during and after reading this book; you will be seen as someone being self-aware, and others will see you showing more confidence than they show, from now on.

**A self-analysis**

Can you see yourself, looking at yourself, seeing inside yourself right now?

Take a minute, and see inside yourself. – Get to know your inner-self!

Become very self-aware!                                                        4

Now...On a scale of 1 to 100, how aware are you awaken to your inner-self?

At first, small hints of this awareness will appear. Then one day while practicing this self-analyzing-method you'll be stronger with it, seeing everything you do from a (inward, outward) point of view; realizing everything that's happening to you is coming from within you.

One of the most rewarding secrets in life, is knowing exactly how to create strength from within, and teaching it to others. – When others feel your strengths, they will instinctively become attracted to you.

**Here's another vision to see yourself better:**

Your (Body) has a mind, too.

How often do you pay attention to your body speaking to you, and to other people?

"How do I hear my body speaking to me, or anyone else for that matter?" you might ask.

Say for instance when your body is tired, dehydrated, hungry, uncomfortable, hurting, nervous, lustful, hot, cold, excited, active, even frightened. Or it's when you have a certain feeling or desire. There are slight tingles and urges you have to be closer to certain people. You feel inwardly stimulated in some situations. (Use your imagination.)

It's in these moments when your body is speaking to you, and to other people.

Before going any further; let's explore the nature of "Hypothetical speaking."

Hypothetical speaking is something thought of, outside the box; such as supposing or assuming something is similar to a description, but you are taking a different look at it from another angle. Allow your mind to adjust to certain concepts in this book to better understand what's being shown in these visions sometimes.

Now when we say you have to be impregnated like a female injected with male-seeds in order to give birth; Well, feel these ideas being injected inside your awareness for newer comprehensions if you want to give (life) to those possibilities you seek. – And they do come with some-pains. Because when you want certain things, they don't always feel comfortable having them in your life.

Say for instance when you want something you've never had before, you are basically in a position of giving birth (or should we say) you are having birth-pains with that new experience because it's coming inside your world reshaping your lifestyle.

Here's another "Hypothetical." – Just imagine you're walking in the middle of a road carrying a magnet, and there's lots of debris on both-sides. While walking, that magnet begins pulling metal out of the debris sticking to it. Now imagine, you are the magnet and everything in your life is coming to you from your inner-pulling sensation; (or should we say) your inner-magnet.

If you keep this "Magnetic Hypothetical" in mind, you'll know exactly how you're making possibilities happen every day. Because everything you think of, or feel, is the reason you have those possibilities coming inside your lifestyle. – You are drawing them to you!

But sometimes, we miscarry or abandon possibilities before they even begin; because they seem too much to bare for long-term. (It's something we call losing or quitting.) That's when we don't fully grasp the process of real living, giving birth to something new all the time; and we don't know exactly what to do with it, or to it. – But in reality, it's the nature of (giving birth to something new) that shows what successful living is.

– And to all women carrying and having children right now, or thinking of having them in the future, (THANK You!) for contributing to our society; and Congratulations!

So when you see an amazing (pregnant woman), say to her; "Thank you!" because she's reminding us of the sacrifices it takes to bring someone new into our world!"

We are all designed to measure our life through the way we feel about something, no matter what it is! That's the difference between seeing what we're doing versus feeling how we are doing it from within.

Does the statement, "I have a gut feeling" come to mind? That's your body speaking to you. – And if you listen to your body more often, you'll hear it telling you how and when you are getting closer, or losing ground with your efforts. Because, to that which you want done is determined by how much effort you put into accomplishing it.

With this book, you're going to see your own reflection in some people. You will see how you're either creating a great relationship with them, or bad ones. – Most of the time you'll think you're staring-back at yourself with some people. You will feel what they feel, think what they think; and sometimes do what they do.

This is called great communication; seeing eye-to-eye and thinking like-minded. This is how you get asked to work a job, get married to someone, become a friend, etc.

As I was saying: Your body is talking to you all day long; and maybe, you're not listening to it enough. Your mind gets most of the credit for deciding what you want (when it's your body measuring the outcome of everything you do from within. It's your emotions, feelings, and your instincts) explaining the outcome of whatever you do.

Your (body-mind) measures, not judge things. That's what your brain does. It judges things while your body feels the effects of whatever happens to you. – And once you take more notice of what your body is doing, you'll feel it reaching outwardly at other people like it does! "Remember when you want to hug someone, or shake their hand; but you don't?" That's because your mind is denying your body to be part of the communication. Take time-out each day listening quietly to what your inner voice is saying. – It's there, just listen closely.

And here's a question...

What would you say, if you had to guess? Does your mind and body do things together, or do they live separate lives within you?

You should look at your mind and body like a marriage, sort of speaking; because when they act together, you're more successful. But when they act separately, that's how you mostly fail with some of the things you do. And if you're not whole or complete inside, then how can you be complete with anything outside you?

Are you more AWAKE to yourself now?

**Be at Peace inside yourself!**

Here's something you are doing, but don't know it. And in order to take more notice of it; relax and notice yourself instinctively feeling outwardly at things around you. – Look at anything, or anyone. You'll feel something pulling your awareness towards it, like your comprehensions is naturally being drawn to it like a magnet.

For instance: Can you feel something inside making you want to brush your teeth, wash your face or hands, get dressed, prepare for a meeting, do dishes, go to work, make money, pay a bill (or just spend some money), exercise, empty trash, watch television, find something to eat, clean the house, read, do homework, go dancing, write your own book, take a bath, make phone calls, play a game, drive a car, contact a friend or loved one, get closer to someone you think likes you; or just fix or repair something? (Use your imagination.)

These activities are filled with your creative energies. The only difference between these things above and everything else you do outside them, is they are natural instincts; and you do them without putting much effort, because they are natural to you!

By staying aware of this, you will see yourself staying away from laziness on all levels.

There's always something tugging on your awareness to do something, no matter what it is. That's why you're always doing something for yourself, and with other people. – It's like you're inwardly reaching outward to do more than what you're doing, all day long.

– Do you notice when certain people come around; you feel a slight tug on your feelings for them? Well, it's true, they are feeling you too. (This is called, Natural attraction.) Your body wants to do something with them; (Use your imagination) because your body, and their body is communicating instinctively in that moment. – Just think about that! – It's okay to have this connection with other people. It's a natural behavior.

Sometimes, you and certain people have an instant connection with each other. But you don't fully know what to do in that moment, so both parties ignore those feelings causing them to fade away; leaving you in the state of assuming what could have been for the rest of your life.

7

And since your mind gets more credit for what you do, it causes so many possibilities to be missed-out on with certain people because of not including your entire being with the communication.

A simple hug or hand-shake could have been used for a greater communication.

A lot of communications are denied or lost because of no hugs or embrace. People measure their interest with you from the way they think and feel about you. They even measure their relationship with you through your hand-shake, hugs, and even in the way you do things physically.

Physical attraction happens as soon as someone lay eyes on you, (or vice versa.) It's a natural instinct we use to measure and govern our connection with other people.

And when you have a great connections with someone; It feels, good! Because you're having a stimulating connection with them, aren't you?

And you should always have this (effective connection) at all times; especially with the opposite sex, because this is what causes you to be Attractive with deeper insights and emotional connections from the things you do with people, all day long.

Do you say to yourself every day; "I love who I am … I love the people I know... I love the things I do?" – This is a natural mindset you should have all day long.

Once you completely wake-up seeing yourself doing these things all day long; you'll have more fun with people and things you do. You'll feel yourself removing laziness, doubts, or any other discomforts from yourself; it will be more natural once these visions become a daily practical routine.

You'll become "very fond of living" while applying these visions to your life every day.

– All of those negative thoughts you have concerning certain people will disappear from you. You won't feel that battle inside you, any more. Your inner-war will end!

**You must learn to express your life from deep within.**

Here's something else you must wake-up to. People around you take more notice when they have a feeling for you. – It's not about how well they listen to you, alone. They can relate better when they are feeling you instinctively and emotionally, or even physically.

Take for instance when you're in a new relationship: You and that person spend more time together by the way both of you feel and interact with each other, don't you?

Even when parents put faith in their child when they're ready to leave home for good; they don't just measure their child's feelings toward life, they are more in-tuned with knowing how their child feels about themselves, and the way they will interact with people in different situations.

Now. From this time forward, don't just rely on your mind alone; allow your feelings and instincts to help condition the things you do. Feel yourself instinctively and emotionally pulling people toward you, or pushing them away.

If you want help understanding this pushing and pulling feeling, just get two magnets and flip them around opposite of each other, then you'll feel exactly what this means.

Even if you do not want to believe you have this deep magnetic power because of fear or phobias, at least notice how you're being pulled to another person, or pushed away from them. You'll still absorb this same on-going sensation, but without your control of it.

This awareness is how you create stronger-relationships with people, whether it be for intimacy with someone you care about, better job relationships, friendships, a business venture, or whatever. – People naturally feel your intentions; they know if you are aware of your actions with them or not. It's the nature of feeling safe with you. All of this power and influence comes from within you, naturally.

**See if you can agree with this vision:**

Every one of us is looking at, and listening to the same things every day; but what makes it different is how we're interpreting things altogether. Say for instance when it rains, some of us see a dreary day. Then there are those of us seeing it from the trees, grass, and flowers point of view. They need rain just as much as we do, even more-so, because they need to live as much as we do. And who's going to give them water?

We each have our own views about life, but it's how we interpret whatever happens around us, and to us.

Just imagine feeling cool-wind blowing; then it gets colder, making you feel the need to put more clothing on to protect yourself from what you consider to be cold-weather. Every time you get colder, you immediately think about warmer clothing. Your body needs this cold temperature. That's why it's here!

Have you ever considered the cold weather may be trying to embrace your body to feed your cells with more oxygen so you can continue functioning alive and healthy?

Also when you are starting a new-relationship with someone; you should make them feel warm inside so they will come to you without hesitations, because this causes them to feel they are walking with the warmth of the "Sun" while being in your presence.

And if you stay aware of these visions, you'll do things you've never done before; you'll be more productive and more inclined to work with people as a team, by understanding everyone everywhere you are, the way you are designed to be.

Here's something you see others doing everywhere, but most people don't know they're doing it. (We all have) the same voices speaking inside us.

Voices, such as:

I want someone I can trust, and they can trust me.

I truly want to express my love to someone, and have them express their love upon me.

I want a happy home; living in a caring, safe, and productive environment.

I'm ready to make sacrifices for those worthy of my sacrifices.

I want to create an inheritance and leave it for future generations to come. Namely, my children's children.

I want loving-soul-mates; such as friends, family members, business acquaintances, lover(s), etc., in my life every day.

I want fun and happy loving people in my life on a regular basis.

I want to be viewed as being socially equipped, and sexually attractive.

And the list goes on and on. (Use your imagination.)

So the question now, is: Are you going to stay awake to the realities that each of us have for the same reasons – no matter who, or what we are?

And aren't you asking (whatever faith) you believe-in, for the same things as everyone else – cars, trucks, clothes, foods, houses, good jobs, successful business? (Use your imagination.)

Hypothetically speaking. – What if, one day, you found yourself alone on this planet with no one else around to love, trust, or believe in you anymore?

Would you be able to abandon these opportunities that are in front of you today? Would there be values in your life if no one else is around to care for you anymore? Don't you know, you're the cause of some people feeling neglected, frustrated, resentful, angry, selfish, loved, sexually-attractive-to you, etc.?

First of all, let's define something you may, or may-have not considered before now.

People are your biggest Asset on this planet. – Without people, you will never succeed in any areas of your life. And you know, this is true!

Your success will always be determined by how big your cheering section is, and how well you turn your options into opportunities!

Some readers of this book might say – "but what do you mean by turning my options into opportunities – let alone, having a cheering section?"                    10

<u>Your options</u> are all those people and things you see in front of you <u>to choose from</u> every day. – And your cheering section is those large groups of people you sometimes go around, for whatever reasons. Or, it could be those small groups that help you, like support groups. Or it could be that one person you hear about that has lots of money, power, and influence. (Use your imagination.)

**Here are some quotes to think about on a regular basis**.

The more you have, the more you're heard.

The more you understand, the more you'll be understood.

What one person won't do, many others will.

Try to avoid putting 100% of reliability in one person; just put 10% in Ten people at a time. – This way, you are still guaranteed 100% of giving from people, and will see they don't mind giving this much of themselves to you. – It's a fact! People give 10% of their earnings all the time – whether it be their time, money, or whatever.

That's all you are getting from people anyway. Just look real closely at that statement. – (Maybe one or two people) will try to give more of themselves to you. And this could be an exception to the rule of it; because when you put 100% of reliability in one person, the outcome of it does not match your belief in them, nor does 100% match-up to the belief others put in you either.

That's what it means, when you hear; "Don't put all your eggs in one basket."

Now, 10% means a lot to those giving it, verses those not giving you anything at all.

And if you're not getting the results you want from people where you are right now; then change cites, change states, or just go live in another country. There are about 7-billion people on the planet and be assured; there is someone out there waiting for someone exactly like you to come into their life.

Once you learn to appreciate the "People Wealth" you already have, that's when you'll feel richer and wealthier than anything you have ever known. – Just think about that!

One of the greatest value you have on this planet is being with people who really enjoy your company, offering and seeking your support.

Invest in "People" then you'll have wealth and riches beyond your greatest dreams. When you really look at this fact, you'll see how success is really achieved. Again, your success is determined by how big your cheering section is.

While you're in this mindset, you see that there's no lacking in any area of your lifestyle.

Now – that's Wealth. That's real Enjoyment, that's true Happiness, that's real Success, and that's true Prosperity.

Think about that water-fall mentioned earlier. "Do you feel More of this down-pour coming inside you now?" – Once you have these visions embedded deeply inside your awareness – you'll possess the "nature of having, continuously" because the streams of continuation and progress will flow inside you all day long, every day.

We all know that there are people creating ways to help society become a better place to live, for the most part. And there's a lot of people truly succeeding, financially. And this is good – very Good!

But still, money alone will not solve humankind's greatest problem, because money will someday fade away – but no time soon. And yet, we still use money to try and out-live any situation there is.

There's a television show I would like to call to your attention. It's called "Star Trek." These people are very highly skilled space travelers. All they're mainly concerned with, is keeping that spaceship flying safely across different galaxies. Money had no value on their ship. The main value they showed were the energy-field, weapons, team-work, and medical-room functioning correctly. – Come to think of it, they never showed the importance of food or eating healthy either. (But that's something we knew they needed.) They mainly showed what it's like keeping everything functioning correctly and thinking healthy. And that's the nature of this book. "Keeping you functioning properly and thinking healthier!"

Again, a lot of people are truly working to help humankind become better people, and money is one of our major surplus for doing that; and true Wisdom and Understanding is now beginning to surface – especially with books like this one.

**Everyone will break free, and here's how**.

One day, in the very near future, "no one" will live admiring someone else's fortune, because true Wisdom and Understanding will be spoken to everyone. And to those who are spending most of their time listening to other people's success; the time is coming when everyone will have the instructions, disciplines, and corrections for fulfilling their own life with prosperous living conditions. No one will have to be singled out, as to say who's success is better than the next person.

But then and again, Who's to say, whose success is better than the next person? And yet, there is proof, evidence, and results from those who do evaluate their income and outcome status with a very successful lifestyle in today's world.

Here's a thought...

Now this might hurt your ego a little-bit, but you'll get over it quickly once you see the point being made. – And it's better to be kicked in the ego for a moment than to keep getting kicked in the gut for the rest of your life – wouldn't you agree?

You cannot stop Wisdom and Understanding from doing their works, no matter who you are, or what you think and do. Life wasn't created by you! – And life as we know it, is not coming to an end; it's still moving in the direction it intended, preparing paradise for us all. – Only those with true Wisdom and Understanding see this.

Remember when you see or hear about disasters, and there are people that survives it? – Well, only those applying Wisdom and Understanding to their daily life will survive any kind of disaster known to humankind.

Those human disasters like, worrying, the cost of living rising, separations on all levels that mankind experience are no different than any earthquake, hurricane, tornado, or any other anxiety we have. Those anxieties that humankind created are only smaller scales of disasters, that's all. – And a lot of people, do survive it!

During and after reading this book, you'll feel yourself removing those man-made disasters you once endured and served. No more feeling alone, lost, empty, or denied your true identity or purpose from this point forward.

Keep thinking about that water-fall filling your comprehensions with the down-pour of these visions, giving you more to change the way you look at things, and see how things are naturally changing before your very eyes.

Don't tell yourself or others that there isn't "Plenty" to go around. Start looking at life filled with Abundance and see how to collect your fair-share of everything you want.

Do you see all those people around you appearing lonely? Do you see all those cars, trucks, houses, clothing stores, grocery stores with untold amounts of food in them? Do you see all those electronic and material gadgets everywhere you look? Do you see so many people with money making any purchase they choose in those stores of all kinds?

See life offering you these abundance every day, and so much more!

Isn't everyone, who wants it, entitled to their-fair-share of wealth, happiness, love, and prosperity? – Yes, we, are!

Because everyone shares the same sunlight, darkness, pains, hungers, guilt, lusts, and desires; but only at different times, in different places, and with different people. But it's all the same, right? – Again, it's all in how we interpret everything.

And everyone shares the same information and knowledge of the world in general. – But, not everyone is sharing the "Wisdom and Understanding" you are reading right now. If they were, the world would seem much different than it is right now, right?

While you're reading this book, you're learning how to obtain more riches, glory and honor, because you're waking-up to wisdom and understanding, removing those blocks that once prevented you from seeing all these riches you so deeply desire.

13

These visions are breaking you-free, to seeing more than you've ever seen before.

While you have spent many years believing in the world of information, only to discover that it's basically filled with many tricks and magic acts, if you stay locked inside its grips of illusions.

Now see wealthier-living conditions that brings more life to breathe better, to see better visually, that will enhance your ability to physically attract those you seek closer to you – even design better financial habits for a more enriching future.

You are in a time of life where anyone who wants success can have it, and master it. Also teach it to others.

Here's a word that alludes many people; and that word is "Subconscious" and so many books mention it, in them. But not many have a very clear definition of its true meaning.

It really means, "Your hidden mind." It's where you collected knowledge of the past, more or less, – a memory-pool of thoughts stored in the back of your mind where a lot of what you did is kept; (some good, and some bad.) Only you know the extent of either.

**Question:** If you looked deep inside your memories, would you say your thoughts and behaviors of the past are like they're in a filing cabinet, or a garbage pile?

That's how you end-up saying things like, "What made me say that?" – "Oh … I see what that means, now!" – "I forgot about that!" – "What was I thinking?" – "Are you sure, maybe!" and the list goes on and on. (Use your imagination.)

When you truly wake-up to Wisdom and Understanding (like you are doing right now); you'll begin remembering hearing yourself speaking those voices above, and others.

Other voices like; "Why don't people show that they really care about me? What's wrong with people, why won't they show me more love and understanding? Why don't people just talk to me, I'm ready for them?" And you have other voices in your head like it, right?

(This part, you may not want to hear.) But it's true!

Maybe, (if this is the case) those voices in your head is misleading you, causing you to think (stupid-wise) to yourself – let alone, thinking (stupid-wise) about everyone else around you. And you might-not know the difference.

Here's how to see if this is true...

Go back a few days ago … See if you wasn't thinking, or said something out of context to someone? Peek inside those memories you have … And go back to any jealousy or anger you had with certain people.

If you look even closer, you'll see that you didn't put true Wisdom or true Understanding in your thoughts, nor spoke it from your lips; (if this is the case.) You thought, or said something very strange concerning people in general. – And still, some people stick around because of how they feel about you.

Here's something to see!

Every thought you have, is either pulling you toward living a better lifestyle, or pushing you away from it … or it's just keeping you standing still like it did in the past.

And remember this: You can't call the truth, a lie!

Another reminder:

No matter who you are (male or female; young or old) you're still being impregnated with the things in life; it's basically how you interpret the birth-pains of it. – Especially, with those anxieties of limitations, lacking, failures, and moments of emptiness in your life (if this is the case.) And you are still living with those anxieties in your life today?

And here's how to know if you are...

If you are telling people what you think they want to hear; you're speaking with illusions, mirages, and ticklings of the ear. You are not speaking true wisdom and understanding to them. And believe this fact – people can tell if you are lying to them, they know from personal experience of doing it themselves. Everything is a mirror reflection to what's true, or false.

Everything you say and do, makes up the process of elimination. No matter where you are, or who you're with – it's all, still the process of elimination.

Let me explain it in more detail...

You see, wherever you are, someone is listening closely to determine if you are telling the truth or not. And by definitions, you are being seen as if you're a person that can fit-into their way of living or not. And if you don't act the way they expect, then you're automatically denied their fan-club, sort of speaking. And if you are doing it to others, then you're the one processing and eliminating them.

And if you're meeting the expectations of other people, then you're being welcomed, greeted, supported, accepted, blessed, and cared-for while seeing the proof, evidence and the results of them feeling this way toward you.

During your quest to discover what real living is, you must realize life isn't really about finding or searching for anything. It's mainly about "Tuning-in-to things" because everything you want is already here to do whatever you want with it. It's basically how you "Tap" into its existence and be magnetically pulled to it like a magnet, naturally (like you did with this book.)                                                              15

## How to tap into the existence of something?

The first thing to do, is awaken to its existence knowing that it already exists.

Second thing to do, is to let it fill your mind and emotions with as much of its existence as you can, without hesitation.

Third thing to do, is knowing how far away, or how close you are to it.

Forth thing to do, is notice its presence developing inside your lifestyle.

Fifth thing to do, is not just think about it; have a relationship with it so it will happen with time and your efforts. (A mental relationship can easily creates a physical relationship with anything.) – Feel it happening to you, Now!

When you start Tapping into the things you want out of life, you'll feel the sensations of what you want drawing closer to you like a magnet.

And remember, everyone you are searching for, is also searching for you.

Also, the more people you talk to, the better your chances are for success. You never know who might be carrying that missing piece of the puzzle you're looking for.

Do you feel how much easier it is attracting things to you now? You must keep this magnetic mentality turned-on inside your awareness at all times, and never turn it-off!

Keep feeling as though you're "Tapping Into" the existence of things you want. Put more feelings into it, and pull with your emotions. Feel like a magnet pulling metal to it. Even now, you feel these magnetic sensations getting stronger inside you.

And remember, it takes wisdom and understanding to live a fun-filled life of giving all the time. So, when you see someone being interested in you, know that you're magnetically drawing them to you, (or vice versa.) That means, deep down inside them you're fun to be with.

It's a small pulling sensation at first; but the more you're awaken to this feeling you'll become stronger with it. Whether it's for a job interview, a marriage proposal, an enjoyable date, a business venture, or whatever. (Use your imagination.)

Realize, that this magnetic sensation gets stronger and stronger every time you apply it to any situation. So stay awake to it and accomplish whatever you want with more ease.

Your inner-magnet works much better with (people) than it does with inanimate objects; but it does work, no matter the reason you're using it for. It's mainly the Life of Attraction and Cause of Effectiveness at work here, instead of The Law of Attraction.

And if you choose to call it the Law of Attraction, then that's okay. Some people have spent years learning that meaning. And yet, it's all about living A Life of Attracting things to you when everything is said and done.

Some words seem harder to relate to, because of the way they are used.

Say for instance: When you hear people say; we only use one-tenth of our brain (which is an insult if you really think about it!) But if you do research on that statement, you will discover the real message was; we only use one-tenth of our language, because most words when trying to pronoun them seem like a whole new language.

The same goes for (The Law of Attraction.) It's really (The Life of Attraction) if you really looked at its true meaning. Which seems bigger, and more effective.

Look at Life itself, first – then look at some (Law) that might work for you? – But you be the judge of it!

The more awaken you are to this fact, the wiser you'll become with it.

Also while you're feeling these visions entering your body-mind, It's removing everything related to poverty, hard-times, separation on all levels, limitations, struggles, and stress causing situations out of your life; especially right now.

It might feel kind of slow right now; but still, you are feeling those forces in and around you that were keeping you broke, lost, denied, lied-too, hurt on many levels, loosening their grip and going away forever.

Again, this book is about seeing true wisdom and understanding working in your life. But, from time to time, you'll feel how easily it is having more of everything you want. Because with these insights, anything you want can be drawn to you, and money is no different than anything else. Your inner-magnet works everywhere you direct it, and will be accepted by any pulling sensation within your visual and emotional reach.

And isn't life much better being an example for others to see?

Just look at what happens to role-models, great mother and father figures, and leaders of all kinds; they enjoy being loved, respected, supported by loved-ones, friends, and acquaintances. Life seems to work in their favor all the time. They live in the lime-light of their existence; don't they?

Here's something to support those statements...

When great role-models think about having "more" of anything; they think how it feels having more of what they want, (not need.) They use their instincts to "touch" its energy and hold it with everything they got, every day, everywhere they are.

It's like they have an inner-magnet instinctively pulling people and things to them. And that's what you've been doing too, but wasn't truly aware of it, until now!

Just look at the people and things you have in your life right now. There's the proof, right there in front of you. – Are you beginning to see how everything come to you now?

Everything you have, came from having that inner-magnet inside you. And everything else you get will be done the same way. (Some of it will be Slow, and some will be Fast.) But, it all depends on how strong your inner-magnet is that make things come to you quicker. The stronger your inner-magnet is, the quicker you get results.

And if you want to call it faith or hopeful living; then that's entirely up to you! – Either way, you'll still be able to check the status of your life each day with these visions.

And these visions will always be a reflection of what you are doing now, and what you will be doing in the future.

As you can see, "Wisdom and Understanding" doesn't need a control switch like society has, and always will try to do. It want us to serve their purpose voluntarily. And we want their power of insights guiding us all-day-long if we truly value successful living.

And isn't it time to have real knowledge giving real results to your efforts when you are comprehending it; results to your life that cannot be disputed or denied no matter what else is being said or done about it?

And isn't it time to have knowledge that provides more prosperity, than just hope; not stringing you along, tickling your ears? You want proof, evidence, and results to real living; not made up stuff! – You want answers and solutions to real living, right now!

Now you can see the truth of "Wisdom and Understanding" in and around you.

But before taking a look at this fact, allow a place of proof where their existence came from that cannot be thought of being something made up by the author. – By reading these verses, you're not being asked to become religious or anything. You are just being shown the proof, evidence, and claim of their existence – nothing more at this point. Everything else you believe or don't believe is up to you.

**Proverbs** (1:20-31), (2:3,4), (4:7-9), (7:4), (8:11-36), (9:1-6.) Read these verses to better understand the next point being made here.

Now. Just imagine two "living beings" hidden from the naked-eye, escaping society's awareness, roaming in our mist going unnoticed by people all day long. And these two mighty being have with them great knowledge, wealth, and true power, waiting for us to accept their proposal. Watching and waiting for anyone who wants true power and great influence.

What do we do?

Do we accept this proposal, or do we continue ignoring this offering like most of society does every day, not having any awareness of their existence at all?

Now that you are aware of this; no matter what else you do from now on, you'll silently hear their voices offering you knowledge to better living conditions.                    18

And you might ask: "So why didn't I know of this before now?"

The best way to explain it, is this way ...

You. Along with the (Powers to Be) together, with your many voices of doubt, worries, lies, tricks, selfishness, ego, and other illusions existing inside your mind, created that mental blockage you had.

These illusions keep most people from being happier, joyful, loving and supportive to others, prosperous, and healthy. Causing most of society to live ignoring any true efforts concerning happier living conditions for everyone.

The (Powers to Be) exists within the realm of the unseen controlling the seen. And so does Wisdom and Understanding. We each must make the right decision to improve our lives individually.

...Now choose? – The (Powers to Be), or (Wisdom and Understanding?)

Do you mentally hear, or emotionally feel them revealing themselves to you now?

– "Yes... A little," you might say?

Well keep reading and absorbing these insights and you'll see or feel them more clearly.

You can instinctively feel or hear them if only you remove that veil (blind-spot) from over your awareness and truly notice their existence.

And, isn't this a good time to start listening to them personally now? Or, are you going back to that lost, blind, threatening lifestyle you call living – to those things in life making you feel egotistical, selfish, naïve, arrogant, spiteful, jealous, confused, angry, or just foolish?

Here's another question... Do you feel like a Volunteer in your life, or a Victim to it?

A Volunteer choose from the options they have in and around them. – And a Victim is one of circumstances. To them, things just happens and they go along with it.

Victims think things happen because of their situations, and can't do anything about it. They think they are caught inside a Labor Chamber working themselves to old-age; so they feel their circumstances are much bigger than their choices.

But there are those choosing to do things based on enjoyment and excitement, thrills, great interests, or whatever; (Use your imagination.)

But the truth is: Your life is based on how well you connect to the "Unseen" controlling the "Seen" for the most part. – Just think about that!

If you look closely at people, you'll see everyone having the same thoughts and feelings you have, basically at the same time. – Only being where you are right now and the people you're with, determines whether these statements are true or not.          19

– Being in the right place, at the right time is the truth to it all.

Look at the way you make connections with certain people. (Yes a lot of what you have is from having certain values to exchange for products or services.) But still, the outcome of whatever you have is from how well you interacted with other people.

It's how well you make connections with someone that's out of the ordinary for the most part. You see, most of us are conditioned to believe in some sort of faith that works in our favor. (Which isn't a bad thing.)

**But truth be told**; Why isn't faith or prayers working the way we want them too?

Is it faith, itself? Or should we start considering that maybe, our prayers and faith is selfish and don't see how much it involves other people, places, and things? And when you pray (if this is the case); are you thinking your prayers and faith has to serve, only you?

So if you pray, see the bigger picture of other people being involved; then your prayer stands a better chance of being answered. – Just a thought!

Here's another question to answer:

Are you standing-still in your life? Or are you actively creating better living conditions for yourself and future generations to come?

And you might say;

"How could I just be standing-still when I'm always on the go, working, making all kinds of meetings, and things like that?

This injection will show if you are either standing-still, or actively creating better ways of living for yourself, and others.

Again, it's better to be kicked in the ego for a short period, than to continue being kicked in the gut for a lifetime.

Before seeing the world of Standing-still, let's look at the world of Merry-go-rounds, first.

Each of us enjoys a merry-go-round because they are fun. But there's a time when we want to get-off it, right? The way the merry-go-round works in our lives is from doing the same things over-and-over again. (If this is the case); aren't you tired of living like that?

Why repeat the same things every day; going-around in circles, getting nowhere like you're standing-still in the same conditions in life, year-after-year?

Here's how... (if this is the case.)

If you're still paying the same bills every month, buying the same amount of food each week, driving the same vehicle year-after-year, living in the same house (renting or owning), wearing the same clothes, making the same amount of money every day, having a hand-full of friends or loved ones; then you are standing-still, or going around in circles with your life getting nowhere fast; and life is too short to live under those conditions when there is so much "More" for you to do and have.

Do you not see all those available people, empty houses, car-lots, boats tied to the peer, planes with empty seats, and banks on almost every corner, clothing stores, food stores, and untold gadgets in your visions every single day, waiting for your attention?

And please don't tell yourself, money is the reason you're not getting those things you want! Don't let money be more valuable than your life. Just look at all those people who passed-away leaving their money behind; they are gone, and their money is still being passed around to others.

There are so many people living very large and never worked a day in their life. If I had to make one hard guess at how that happened to them, I would immediately say; Wisdom and Understanding handed-it to them, because they are receptive to being instructed, disciplined, and corrected with the way their life should be.

And by being aware of this, you're seeing abundance flowing to those understanding it.

Listen to this cliché; "The more I have, the more I'm heard;" should be one of your daily affirmation. Simply because you're in a time for having abundance at your disposal.

You should see More, hear More, feel More, and do More with your life. – This is the lifestyle you search for anyway, right? – So tune-in-to it!

But if you're naïve or selfish with having more, just for yourself – now look at your residence, or place of business (job or ownership) and see how much you have has become junk-piles in certain areas. And that's because you wanted more but didn't have invested reasons for having "more" in the long run;

"See...? Look at that big pile you have accumulated? (If this is the case.)

Having "More" means "more" than what you think it is. When you want more things, you must put invested reasons for having it. – If not, then you're stuck with accumulating more junk-piles.

Here's a question:

Which of two choices can you say? "I have "more" than what I need." Or, "I don't have enough to help other people in need?"

Even when you hear of someone that's made a great name for themselves, it's not really about knowing that person; (well, for the most part it's not.)      21

But it's mainly thinking what opportunity revealed itself to give them all the money and power they have.

– It sounds extraordinary hearing about someone having "more" than what they need on a large scale, because most people have no clue how to have things on that level. It's too high, or out of their reach to even think about it.

It's like staring at the moon, wondering how to get there without the help of NASA Space-station. Only astronauts have that privilege. The same can be compared to getting rich. Some people think they cannot get rich without knowing someone already rich.

But that's not true. – Well, for the most part, it's not!

Being wise and understandable is a sure way of tapping into the world of wealth and riches. In other words; (it's having that magic Genie existing inside you.) Because truth be told, our faith and beliefs can work for us, if we use it correctly.

Don't let anything keep you from being connected with your true inner-Genie.

And here's why!

Every day, you look for people, places and things to give you proof, evidence, and the results of knowing how life operates. And you know from personal experiences that your success was and is governed by appointments made with people of similar interests.

If you really think about it, you can immediately grow your life faster; simply by making a lot more appointments with people of similar interests – beginning; Now!

Isn't this the way accomplishments are made anyway? Such as weddings, employment, parties, or any other celebration you prepare?

And remember, the more appointments you make, the more options you will have to turn into opportunities. – Keep thinking about "People Wealth" while you are at it.

You don't have to wait for people to set appointments with you; you can set personal appointments with people instead. (Create your own success schedule, every day.)

Set-up more appointments and see what happens? You already know how this process work. It's always successful when someone agrees to meet with you. And that's also the "Process of elimination." You stop going in circles doing the same old things; and you're removing stagnations and stand-still moments from your life as well.

Some of you might say: "But what if I don't have a phone or car to make appointments?" There are no excuses! (You're thinking with fear and phobias) like you did in the past.

"Change the way you look at things, and the things you look at will change!" *By Dwight Dyer*

Everyone goes through life searching for that special someone, or something amazing to happen to them. In other words, waiting for that magic moment or magic-Genie to come to our aid. That's why we search (or should we say) try to "Tune-in-to" the realm of "Spirituality" as a means of having (these blessings) coming to us from time to time.

But nothing is more rewarding than expressing Wisdom and Understanding all day long, having your deepest desire staring back at you, and always seeing something different waiting for you to take action toward it everywhere you are. So don't search for anything else any more. – Just tune-in-to whatever you want to have!

If you really want to attract any person you desire, just let them see their own reflection in you, and you'll see them being drawn to you naturally.

And how do you do that, exactly?

When you are with someone you enjoy; let them see you feeling the same way they feel. – Look at them, and speak like you know they are ready for a great conversation, a hug, a kiss, or whatever; even an exchange of phone numbers for later communication. (Use your imagination.) Either way, it's still an appointment with them – and you could also be the answer to their prayers!

Become a mirror reflection to others – act like you know how they feel and what they want; because you have the same expectations they have. – And we all know, everyone loves looking at themselves in a mirror from time to time; don't we?

Only when others see a reflection of themselves in you, they become attracted, and vice versa; you'll feel the same attraction with them.

All a person want, is reasons to be with you. And being wise and understandable is a very good reason.

Now say to yourself; "I have every reason to attract any one I want, to me!"

This should be your first thought because you have good reasons to attract any one you want to you. – This naturally makes people draw close to you.

**Seeing into your future**

How do you see yourself in the future?

Are you standing at a podium teaching others how to become successful?

Are you owning, or running a striving business, leading others productively?

Are you preparing to pass-on an inheritance to future generations?

Are you inventing great ideas to help humankind become better people?

Are you a very wise and understandable person?

Are you are a person with great power, and great influences?

At this point, you should hear People thinking things like; having dinner, seeing a movie, being intimate, maybe marriage and children, business venture, or whatever. (Use your imagination.) – These desires are always inside people's minds every day; there's no need to plan anything from here. Just show you understand what people are expecting out of life – and stay aware of these expectations every day, all day long.

So make greater use of your abilities and see how much people really want to do those things above. Keep your awareness filled with this abundance. And it doesn't matter if no one say anything about it; but be assured, they are definitely thinking it. Just act like you are responding to the expectations within their mind, and see what happens?

And remember: If you want to know how smart you really are, look behind you and see how many people are following. (Your success is always determined by how big your cheering section is.) At the same time, make sure you know what kind of people are following you. This makes you keep an eye on those truly supporting you while moving forward to successful living. – Always know where you are, and who you are with.

**How to tell when A Purpose show up**

We are all involved with some kind of plan in one way or another. But when a purpose show up, that's when things really get interesting. – The things we had in mind at first become something greater than what we had imagined. And when we hear people tell us to make a plan, they are basically asking us to layout a course of action to follow. – It does make sense to have a step-by-step procedure. And that's if you follow the steps according to plan. –But you will learn, that a plan is only good until a purpose shows-up.

When setting plans, you are putting a lot of things together. Initially, some portions of a plan does provide life to it. But still, when you are actively putting a plan together, those little things that wasn't thought of at first starts showing-up inside your comprehensions.

Little ideas and details of a purpose starts emerging, causing the planner to rethink the outcome of things.

This is why a lot of plans fall-wayside to planners, because they won't let the purpose of their plan come to the surface. – There's always more to a conversation than what's being said. (And never forget that!)

When people start a plan, they are very interested in what might-be in that moment. Then the purpose (or should we say) the reason for making a plan start flowing inside their thoughts, emotions and feelings with a pulling sensation of a Purpose like gravity pulling existence in place.

One way to notice a Purpose taking place is seeing a Man and Woman being drawn to each other. – We all know what happens when these two make great connection with each other. Especially if love and happiness is assisting their encounter.          24

The continuation of humankind's existence is established by this purpose.

At first, dating, phone calls or regular meetings occur. Then out of the ordinary, they start performing the purpose (or reasons) for being together. (Use your imagination.) And if you understand human relationships, then you know exactly what's being applied here.

And you became a purpose to humankind the first day you were conceived.

**More on the subject of having a Plan:**

A plan is something made mainly for planners. There's no room for anyone or anything else until the planner knows the outcome of their own efforts, first – then other people and things will be considered.

Now you might say; "But don't people come together with Plans?"

Yes. Planning does have its advantages – but mainly for the ones making the plan.

But a Purpose has more significance to it – and here's why.

Life as we know it, is a Purpose; not something planned. Even though some people think getting married, having children, preparing a party or other celebrations, business ventures, dates, or whatever, is something you plan. – It's still a Purpose. Not a plan!

A lot of people look at life from a planning perspective, not a purpose. And here's how to see that. – If you look closely at yourself – which would you consider being done mostly in your life?

Were your past accomplishments made from what you planned; or made from what naturally occurs in life? – And when was the last time you heard someone say their success was all due to something they planned? (And if you did, it was an isolated incidence.)

Let's take a closer look at this situation?

Say for instance when you are arranging a meeting with someone for whatever reason. Yes, you may have planned to get with them. But the outcome will always be the same. You and that person came together because of a purpose bigger than both of you, or other people involved.

You are doing it for (the reason of a purpose), nothing less! – No matter what it is.

And everything is connected to purpose. Maybe not for your purpose. It could be for someone else's purpose without you realizing it.

Also remember, this book isn't written to start judging people's plans. It's about waking up, realizing you're "more" than what you think you are – but only if you stay awake measuring yourself with it.

Wisdom help us see way-beyond our present settings, also to understand the settings inside other people's lives as well; and how wise counsel and leadership is created.

And Understanding shows us how to relate to the things we have inside us – how great communication is born.

By having Wisdom and Understanding, you'll see how coming together with people will cause you to live happier and prosperous and leave a great inheritance for future generations to come, and also (keep it in-tact) for them.

Another quote to remember:

"A wise person will leave an inheritance for their children's children."

Once you fully embrace Wisdom and Understanding, it will pull you inside a (deep powerful source of gathering) in life on a whole new level to that which you have never known before, and you will affect anyone in your wake. You'll embrace wonderful things happening naturally everywhere you are, with everyone you meet.

Just by you reading a portion of this book, you are absorbing and embracing an energy that's filling your comprehensions with better living conditions – isn't it? Just think how you'll be in the future with these memories developing inside your mind every day? – You will have the power of influence that will be irresistible.

Most people don't know, whatever they thought or felt in the past, is the outcome of where they are today. And by you reading this book right now, you're going to have a much brighter future because your mind is being filled with memories to a brighter today and tomorrow, which leads to better living conditions in the future.

– That's how life really works!

It's these thoughts and feelings you have today that will always cause you to stand-up and be accountable; and you won't be mistreated or asked to step-back out of the way in the future because these insights are showing you how to come forward from that backstage behavior and be more inspiring and productive in your life from now on.

## How to remove laziness and procrastination...

One way to remove laziness and procrastination, is to realize you have strengths within that hasn't been tapped into, yet. All you have to do is see that emptiness or weakness that won't reveal itself.

If you can just feel something inside you that is not moving, (you'll in a stand-still); so concentrate on it, and it will eventually start moving you toward doing something you should be doing. Your lack of concentration in certain area of your life is why you don't feel the power of movement within yourself. – That why some people spend a lot of time Meditating.                                                          26

They feel themselves standing-still within. They are not satisfied with (just being) (in one spot-settings) in their lives, not developing more steadily.

Keep looking at the way your thoughts are changing and you'll see yourself moving away from laziness, creating a better today, tomorrow, and a much brighter future.

Remove judgments from your mind and measure your way to better living conditions. Don't just say you want more; Feel "more" coming towards you, with your (Mind, Body, and Spirit!)

Look closely, and you'll see how to create the life you want, today. And remember, you are the creator of your own existence now. Life has done its part; now it's your turn to continue the process of it. Don't search outside yourself for anything, keep looking deeper within – that's where all your answers are kept and waiting.

Keep reading, there's so much more to come.

– So let's continue, shall we?

The reason a lot of people cannot see into the future is because they are too busy reliving their past anxieties. Everything they can think of, or say, is about someone or something that happened in their past. There is nothing concrete about a better future with them. Unless, you call putting past issues in front of you and that becomes their future as well. – But isn't that something they've been doing anyway?

They are always reliving their past, living backwards not moving forward, and there's no real future for them! – And doesn't it make sense to realize, that if someone doesn't know where they are going; then why follow them at all?

True wisdom and understanding breaks you free from bondage and captivity in every area of your life. You feel freer, uplifted and enlightened everywhere you are naturally without a doubt!

When you have found; or should we say, *(tuned-in-to)* true wisdom and understanding, there is no shadow of a doubt you've made a great discovery and feel its effects right on the spot. – You feel it right then and now!

You feel inspired and enlightened knowing something amazing is happening to you in this moment because you are projecting new thoughts seeing how to create success. You feel yourself changing like something new came-on inside your awareness.

It's not something you describe. It's something you feel occurring without putting much thought into it, because the energy of something better is growing inside you right now.

You feel the healing sensations of it all. (You feel refreshed.) These are samples of how powerful our bodies are, but most people don't know they have it in them. Because if they did, their lifestyle would-be much better than what it is! 27

Another thing to call to your attention is this...

When you truly wake-up to real living, your expectations comes to the surface of your awareness because you see the proof, evidence, and the results of them being fulfilled. You start recalling how you did things in the past, verses how you're doing things today.

You see, when you recall how you got things done successfully in the past, you start recalling those same steps it took to great achievements and successful living. And when you apply those same applications today, you will notice yourself having the same keys (knowledge and inspirations) for opening doors to living the way you want to live.

A lot of people forgot what they said and did to make success work for them in the past. All you have to do is remember how you were then, and act the same way, now!

Those steps you took to success in the past worked back then – why wouldn't they still work, today?

And here's something to share with you:

"There once was a person who built bridges anytime they wanted to. So one day, that person built a certain bridge, then burned it down. The problem wasn't burning it down – the problem was, they left their tools on the other side of the bridge."

The moral of the story is: Always keep these visions handy so you will know how well they work for you, and easily see how different you are compared to those around you; without a doubt! – Don't forget, with these vision developing inside you – you can build a relationship with anyone you want, whenever, however, or wherever you choose.

And don't let anyone else's expectation push your expectation aside – or you'll have a losing ground feeling, and failure is the result of not holding-up your end of the bargain.

There's one thing that's really missing about our lives everyday; and that is Us, truly not noticing ourselves living life to the fullest each day. We don't truly appreciated who we are, or what we're capable of doing. And once you completely adjust to seeing the proof of these discoveries revealing themselves to you right now, you won't turn back to your old way of thinking any more. –You are newer (no, a better person) now.

By acknowledging these visions all day long, every day; you'll never run out of things to say or do – or never run-out of loving people any more. You'll always be in a continuous spiral of success, not repeating those damaging behaviors of the past. In other words, you won't have those empty blank black-holes inside you, because they won't exists any more.

**Change is taking place everywhere you look...**

Life is filled with changes, and here's why: The seasons change. The weather change. Time changes – and so do we! 28

Everyone has a changing mechanism inside them; (that's why we all change) and how we relate to different seasons and conditions in our lives, also different people. We're basically learning through personal experiences how to adapt to any changes in life, because we all know; things will change without notice if we're not aware of how change naturally occurs in life altogether.

Have you noticed when you're with someone, or doing something, and it's not the same when you come back to it? Well, that's a small application of how change is always taking place. And once you learn to stay aware of this powerful natural occurrence, occurring in and around you all the time; then you'll know how to adapt to anyone or any situation in life. – That's the true nature of overcoming any situation if you really looked at it.

The weather is going to change. People are going to change too. And there is nothing you can do about it, except change with it. Even you are going change, because some of your situations might-not-be to your satisfaction at the time being.

So, wake up and realize; you are naturally a part of any changes occurring around you. You'll see how to be more stable than those who are not aware of this on-going natural process taking place whether you want it to, or not.

There is a rule of thumb to the process of change; (The Temperature) is a reminder to us when the weather is changing. – There's Winter, Spring, Summer, and Fall.

Have you ever considered, that you and everyone else change like the seasons?

Sometimes, people are compliant, non-compliant, agreeable, disagreeable, happy, sad, spiteful, jealous, angry, or bitter with certain people – and even at some-things.

Then you might say: "But isn't that a part of being human?"

Yes it is! – But still, it's you changing like the seasons every time you do those things above. And it all depends on the environment you're in. Your environments has a lot to do with how you feel, and what you're capable of doing at the time being. That's the effectiveness your environments have on you; (if you let it!)

Remember when you hear someone say: "Hanging around certain people will describe who you are? Or, hanging-around rich and successful people will cause you to become rich and successful like them?"

Well. It's true! – You are measured by the people you hang around-with. Just wake-up and notice how your environments are affecting the way you live today.

Then you might say; "How am I affected by those around me? They are doing them; and I'm doing me!"

Here's how (if this is the case.)                                                  29

Just look a little closer and see if you're acting like others right now, not communicating productively? See if you are responding to how they feel about you? Not about your life, but about the one they think you should be living?

Are you getting angry with someone? Are you spending most of your time concerned with what someone else think about you? Are you spending most of your hard-earns on someone or something else, more than your own lifestyle? (Use your imagination.)

If you are doing these things, then you are not doing you – you are doing them and don't realize it! But it's okay if you don't mind doing those things. Just remember, you are doing them, not you!

Any size achievement you have, will be uplifted to newer heights of accomplishments with these visions. Those thoughts and feelings you had of being broke in any form, is being removed from you. You'll never return to that empty, lonely lifestyle ever again.

Just allow time and these visions to work together inside you, and feel your awareness and comprehensions being redesigned. – It's worth it. So don't rush anything to happen fast – let your mind, body and spirit slowly absorb these visions all day long, and you'll see yourself in a whole new light!

**How to connect to the expectations of other people.**

Each one of us are experiencing the same thoughts and feelings every day. And these experiences happen at different times in different places with different people. But still, we have the same cravings and expectations. – Have you ever thought about that?

For instance: All of us experience hunger, get tired and sleepy, show happiness, have empathy, and offer remorse; and even express the negative side of things, sometimes.

When looking closely at humankind, you'll notice everyone searching for that one special celebration they've never had before. Because each of us desire to have that missing piece of the puzzle that completes our life.

That missing piece of the puzzle can be a person, place, or thing that completes us.

Even you, are a piece of the puzzle to someone's life. Just notice how you're naturally being pulled inside every place you visit and by the way you share your personal resources with others; such as your (family members, friends, job, or whatever.)

- ■ You really think you're the one setting up those situations in your life, don't you? But the truth is, everyone has already been designed to be in every place they are. Again, it all depends on how you interpret where you are, at the time. Just like you may be wondering what brought you here reading this book right now.

Life already had this moment in time setup for you to be reading this book. (You've been chosen, because you've always asked for more wisdom and understanding.)          30

And remember, whatever you're searching for is also searching for you. This knowledge is too big for anyone with a small awareness, they cannot comprehend it all.

**The Powers to BE.**

And on this subject, the powers to be are those authority figures and laws making you feel obligated and responsible for your own existence. This is your life; so why are you letting this happen to you? You're the one in-charge of your own existence! You have the understandings of knowing what will and will-not happen for you. (Don't forget that!)

Don't give away your own power to be whoever or whatever you want to be. It's in these times that you are engaged with an unusual force to place certain ideas of yours out into the open to move ahead to whatever you truly want. You have the power to do that!

And since most of the world lives breaking nature's protocols instead of living Wiser and Understandable, many laws are steady being enforced, governing society and rendering the people powerless. – The more each <u>law</u> is used, the more powerful it becomes.

Where there's a law, and it doesn't require your involvement with it; then stay away from it?! – Keep your distance away from as many laws as you can!

And if you look closely at humankind, you'll basically see them moving according to the suggestions of worldly Laws, instead of moving accordingly to Nature's protocols.

Not everyone breaks protocol, or governed by worldly laws because they are wise and understandable concerning the way life works. – Wise people make use of worldly laws by fencing them around their lifestyle keeping undisciplined law-breakers, and Criminals away.

Since so many people live without true wisdom and understanding, society has become a huge arena of law-followers; and wise people have capitalized on them, keeping their lifestyle safer. But at the same time, worldly laws makes life more difficult for those living without wisdom and understanding because of breaking nature's protocol on a daily basis; they don't see the true nature of humankind as a whole.

**How are Protocols broken?** – Protocol means – Procedures or Practices.

When you listen to, or follow worldly-laws, you're drifting throughout your own existence; lost, always on the go, never being anywhere you want to be. It's like being everywhere else but in that moment you're in. You don't feel yourself proceeding with anything substantial because of not living the life you truly want to live.

**Learning about your own existence...**

This should be the number one protocols of your own existence – not for some laws. Especially when you are fulfilling expectations in your own life, and the life of other people; such as your family circle, your job or business, friendships, or whatever – even when you enter stores of all kinds.                                          31

**How to grasp and hold the Expectations of people, easily**...

Whenever you are around someone; act like (you are) standing in (their shoes), looking back (at yourself) with (their eyes), speaking back (to you) with (their voice); conducting a great communication with (their behavior) designed by (You.)

Give them smiles, say something nice about them, hold eye contact with them; and from time to time, show that you feel their vibes. It's like looking in a mirror seeing your own reflection. And this makes people feel more at ease and relaxed with you, easily.

**How to know if you're on the path to successful living...**

For instance; when you are driving and all lights turn green. Or when you're in stores that doesn't require you standing in line. Even when people start speaking to you like never before. And there are times when you just feel everything is going your way. (Use your imagination.) By keeping up with these visions, and others, you're going to live a lifestyle worth really living from now on. – Can you see the path you are on right now?

Here's a short story...

There once was a certain person who walked into a very dark room with lots of people trying to feel their way around. So that person lit a candle – then everyone started looking at that person with the candle, and that person said; "Why is everyone looking at me?"

– Don't be surprised, when all of a sudden, you notice lots of people watching you from now on, because you have awakened to true wisdom and understanding and that's the candle inside you now.

**Reason, Purpose, and Remembering why things happens...**

The reason some people live happier lives than others is because they are reminding themselves that each moment of living must be filled with Purpose; and keeping those Purpose's filled with reasons to happen, is their first priority.

Say for instance, (if this is the case) every time you see yourself running out of money, not having the foods you want to eat, or going in debt, etc. (Each time these things start occurring you see it coming); you must always be ready to prevent these things from happening inside your lifestyle. It could be anything from money, food, people, or whatever. (Use your imagination.)

And this way, you are always preventing yourself from being broke, lonely, or poor! You are always seeing how this is a terrible way to live with all the abundance around you. You must always remind yourself that you have purpose and reasons for not living with a losing ground frame of mind, ever.

When you are running out of something (no matter what it is), it's like watching your life running-out of existence, against the will of life, breaking protocol of all kinds. (If this is the case.) – Think about that! And stop agreeing with the loosing-ground-feeling in life altogether. This (isn't the way life) is meant to be!

**Be A great Communicator and great Companion to everyone**

We all know, everyone wants to do things they've never done before, or be somewhere they've never been.

Does Bars, Nightclubs, Group meetings and places such as that, ring a bell? Because it allows people to find and locate others on their mental and emotional levels. These actions mainly occur if people feel lonely, separated, really-down, or empty inside.

Everyone dream of having special people in their lives; they even dream-of-owning their ideal home, drive vehicles that are safe and economical, wear clothing that describes their best qualities, having financial stability in many areas of their lives, great friends, trusting and loving loved ones every single day for the rest of their life.

Since most of humankind march through life each day without noticing, or- (tuned-in-to) their expectations not knowing they are stuck inside those illuminating illusions, chasing after what might-be, while drifting mentally in emotional darkness steady building inside their minds each day, making them wander about, always on the go to get nowhere fast, not seeing those values within their reach – all because of thinking world-information is better than true Wisdom and Understanding.

Another question remains in the system of things:

Why, when we're with some people we forget all the mental and emotional exercises we practiced for peace and stability – that when something unstable comes along without notice, easily trigger us off our course of understanding ourselves?

Are we all, through worldly-information victims of some kind of "**Schizophrenia?**"

**Schizophrenia means**, a psychotic disorder characterized by loss of contact with the environment, by noticeable deterioration in the level of functioning in everyday life, and by disintegration of personality expressed as disorder of feeling, thought as (delusion), perception (as hallucination) and behavior also called dementia praecox; compare paranoid schizophrenia.

So in other words, is society so paranoid that it easily become frightened at the slightest hint of hearing something discomforting going on in our environments that it acts unreasonable most of the time? Has mankind created an enemy within our environment with the help of its host (Us) creating feelings of disorder we have with each other?

Are we letting resentment, doubt, anger, jealousy, spitefulness, and selfishness keep us from building a greater lifestyle for all mankind to enjoy? – And will we continue letting those sneaky hidden-tricks and illusions control our communications with each other?

– It sounds like, this is a self-inflected behavior society brings upon itself!

That's why this book is showing you how to remove those negative forces, (The Powers to Be) in and around you (like shinning bright-lights-on) inside dark places.

You are being shown ways to turn the unknown into the knowing; seeing the unseen become the seen. Your comprehensions lights-up while reading this book; and your awareness of things are definitely being revealed to you.

– And every time you picked-up this book and read it, you feel yourself coming out of that darkness you once served (if this is the case) to better understanding yourself, and the world around you.

Here is something to think about.

Are there voices inside your mind telling you when you've had enough of something, or of someone? Do you sometimes feel something inside you, or about you, dictating the outcome of certain situations with certain people and you're not satisfied with it?

Basically, it's your past behavior battling with your awareness of a brighter future – like One is trying to out-do the other, racing to the finish line, sort of speaking. – Some of the things you are doing today, is trying to convince you to not change so you can continue living the same way you did in the past.

The question now is, do you see yourself doing the same things over-and-over each day; or are you seeing yourself preparing to make changes for a better future?

With these visions embracing your comprehensions, you won't have to keep doing the same-old-things over-and-over again; nor keep living in a stand-still lifestyle either.

The reason so many people fail at planning, is because their expectations run parallel to someone else's expectations. If another person's expectations is getting more attention, then that's because their expectations is showing more promise than yours.

Believe it or not; this will cause you to put less time developing your own plans. Your expectation seem lesser than other people's expectations because of the importance of it, or the lack therein yours. A losing ground feeling occurs, and failure is the result of it.

Now, make sure your expectations is in alignment with the next person's expectation in order to have a great relationship with them. Otherwise, you'll be going down a river without a boat-paddle, sort of speaking. And don't think planning isn't good at this point, but it's better to align your purpose with the expectations of others – no matter where you are, or who you are with!                                                    34

That's how successful relationships are created.

Question?

Up until now, did you ever wonder why you weren't creating thoughts and behaviors to turn the lifestyle you wanted in your favor? Or why you worked so hard trying to keep-up with the economy?

Just stay with me for a moment.

What if you could see yourself giving your life away to someone else's lifestyle? The real you is basically observing yourself outside your own existence every day. – What if you could see yourself handing your mental and physical strengths to help complete someone else's lifestyle, leaving your own lifestyle out the equation of true success?

Are you seeing yourself (if this is the case) living outside your own lifestyle right now? Would you agree that you are maybe, making some serious miscalculations in your life?

Let me be more-blunt for a second.

Now. This is not asking you to stop doing whatever you are doing, or with whomever you are doing it with. – It's just asking if there will be "Plenty" of your lifestyle left to go around to future generations (namely, your children's children) when your life is over.

Those thoughts and behaviors you have right now should convince your loved-ones you have "Plenty" to give them, and also pass-it-onto future generations coming (namely, to their children's children.)

If not, then you're conditioning yourself to believing-in thoughts and feelings of having "enough" that it's your way of living; (if this is the case.) And you believe you only need "enough" for the presence. – But enough is never enough; especially if you are behind on certain payments, in debt, have children, vehicles of any kind, or just have certain dreams and goals you still want fulfilled.

(Are you still with me?) Then you are wiser and stronger than you think you are!

This (is not) about debating or contradicting what's being said. It's about you giving more thought and consideration to the lifestyle you want to live. – If not for yourself, then maybe for those you care about.

As I was saying, the reason for saying you have "enough" has been creating the things you've done your entire life. You may-have put "enough" on so many situations that you cannot tell the different between having enough to fulfill obligations, or doing enough to live a better, more enriching lifestyle to pass-on to others.

Let's go deeper...! Have you ever heard the words; "Living by a code? Or the code of conduct?"

Are you living by a <u>code</u> of "Needing More?" Or living by the <u>code</u> of "Wanting More?"

Wisdom shows how a large portion of society is made to feel they have "enough" just to make ends-meet, every day, each week, monthly, and year-after-year; and people have gotten so used to that, that it seems very challenging, if not impossible, to look beyond that scale of living. And that has become their <u>code</u> of conduct, just needing enough to survive their living standards with certain people and situations they favor.

Wisdom and Understanding takes needing, and enough, out of your lifestyle, teaching you how to live in a state of having "More" and getting it!"

Desperation, puts people in a state of "Needing" what they have. Not really "Wanting" it. Desperation, puts people in a state of thinking and saying "you need this and that, to make ends-meet."

Do you feel your comprehensions widening with the way you look at things? Because, when you look at things now, you see them changing before your very eyes.

From reading this far, you Feel yourself moving away from desperation and needing anything. There is a lot more to have; and all you have to do is want "More" of it.

Don't (feel a need) for anything else. – Start "Wanting More" instead. This breaks that <u>code</u> of needing and puts you in the <u>code</u> of having ["More"] to share.

"Needing" weakens the spirit of having More in your life, whether you believe it or not.

For example: People say things like: "I need a job, for this and that reason. I need to lose weight, for this and that reason. I need more money, for this and that reason;" etc. As you can see, they already have the reason – they should just go about getting things done, instead of needing things to happen; that's all.

Do you see where this is going now?

**This is how life works!**

– When you want something to happen in your life – first, know how to come in contact with your inner-strengths.

And here's how...

The best way to make a reality happen, is to impress an image upon your mind until it becomes scripted in your character, and continue the procedures of taking steps toward manifesting that image, no matter the conditions surrounding you. – Put yourself in a state of completing that image while manifesting it. This make it happen naturally. It's called (mind painting.) Continue the picture in your mind until you are done with it.

To succeed at something; practice-practice-practice, rehearse-rehearse-rehearse. And remember, the more you work at it, and think about it, the quicker it becomes a reality to you. – And this goes for anything you want out of life!                    36

Now really think about this, (If this is the case);

Remember when you are paying rent each month, car payments, budgeting for food, gas, and any other necessity you practice, rehearse, or remember throughout each year in order to keep your situations going smoothly – it's like you are remembering how to play your part in a movie, or holding-up your end of the bargain; isn't it?

Now start seeing yourself applying that same script to the life you want to live today. Start applying the visions that's going to fulfill those expectations you want proof, evidence and results from. –This book gives you newer visions to recreate your lifestyle and so much more. And there's no reason to think otherwise.

So, now it's time to stop living with just "enough." Start having "More" of everything you want, just for the asking.

**On the topic of "Just for the asking."**

You can have anything you ask for if you show sincerity for the support you're getting. Givers want to know if the receiver have good intentions with their gifts. They want to know how responsible a receiver will be with their offerings. Just show that you are going to make their gift an invested venture for more than just yourself.

When you are seeking support for whatever reason, notice how others are watching to see how you act with an opportunity. They watch your character, they listen to your voice to hear truth. They monitor you to see if you're a good candidate for their support.

It doesn't matter if it's your first time meeting them. This goes for all relationships with any person you meet. – They must feel a good connection with you. And if you speak to people like you know what they expect from you, then your encounter with them will be much smoother.

That's why a lot of times, people have second thought, because they don't know you well enough to trust you in that moment, or your intentions.

Haven't you heard about people who can come into a room and immediately get the crowd's full attention, and make them excited? They know how to connection with people. It's natural to them. – Are you like this too?

So, when speaking inventively or softly to people, you cause them to listen with their undivided attention because you are speaking to them, not at them. You are calling to their attention things they can relate to; they don't feel you're trying to take something away from them without their approval. That puts you in a position of receiving their support, easily.

Do you feel the energy of having "MORE, now?"

Always think of having More, so you won't let limitation and stand-still moments rob you of succeeding with newer opportunities coming your way. 37

Think More and break-free from those present captivities that have a hold on you.

Think of having More adventures into the unknown, leaving your present comfort zone.

Think of having More money, More than you ever had.

Think of having More people loving and supporting your efforts in life.

Think of having More friendships.

Think of having More time to do things you haven't done yet.

Feel like you're already receiving More, to give More to those you truly care about.

So let these visions sink-deeply inside your awareness and comprehend what having More of everything really means.

Are you still feeling the down-pour of wisdom and understanding coming inside you right now? – Learn how to see more coming to you?

Now. Take a seed for instance when it's placed in soil; it sits in place until water or moisture comes to make it break-free from its shell. And when it breaks-free to the surface of the soil, sunlight begins nourishing it, making it stronger, turning it into a plant, flower, or tree. And the same apply while you're absorbing these visions inside your comprehensions. You are becoming a more enlightened person now.

By reading this book, you feel yourself growing mentally and emotionally. And in some ways, you're mentally preparing for a better financial and physically-attractive lifestyle.

Here's something else to think about;

What if one day soon, people all of a sudden start treating you better than they ever have? How will you respond to this opportunity? What's the first thing you would do in this situation?

Will you act the way you were before discovering this book; or will you act according to the way this book is showing you to be? Because all of those dreams and wishes you had about being with people, many days, months, and even years ago will suddenly appear in a split-second; and every relationship you ever wanted with people will be in your grasp.

That's why this book is awakening and enlightening you to a better existence today, and for you to pass your lifestyle on-to future generations to come.

Let me explain it this way…

Just by having this book you see a brighter future; not just for you and those you care about now, but also for those coming behind them; (Your children's children.)

– Can you see how wisdom and understanding is showing you more opportunities to a much bigger cheering-section headed your way – even for those you truly care about? – Just think about that for a moment?

And if you don't have someone to love today; just know this, there is someone out there in the world looking for someone exactly like you to love.

One of the greatest success's you'll ever have is knowing what the future holds for you, because wisdom and understanding will teach you exactly what to expect, and the exact way to having a brighter, more fulfilling lifestyle today, and in the future.

These visions are waking-you-up from that dreary lifestyle you once called reality (if that is the case), and start seeing those little things you do, adding up to bigger things to come, socially and economically.

Here's an open-invitation for having a positive connection with people everywhere you are, naturally.

– When someone smiles while walking toward you; stop and say something to that affect, they are naturally asking you to connect with them. They opened themselves for a relationship because your vibes and appearance show an interest they seek, and they are approving you for a relationship with them. (Even if it's for a short period of time.)

Every time you practice greeting people with smiles and small-communication-stops, just think how affective you will be, in time? – So don't forget; Practice makes Perfect!

This is a natural expression people give you, so make better use of this opportunity. Act like you accept their friendly proposal. Let these natural instincts guide you to victory with people of all genders, Male and Female; young and old alike. Live inside the Life of Attracting. – Let it work naturally for you.

**On the subject of Attraction...**

Society has put a lot of laws in the world concerning attraction. They've even put a law on (Attracting, as a whole); like we need a law just to make sense out of Attracting, in general? Attracting is something we do naturally. It's our human instinct, and keeps us fruitful and multiplying, and also for accumulating the things we want in our lives!

Don't take this description the wrong way, because the Law of Attraction does work; but only for those who can relate to it on that level. And not everyone sees the same things happening at the same time.

Now with that in mind: Any man-held-law, can and will be broken at some point in time. – Not to mention the untold amount of laws being broken in the system every single day by those thinking they are above or below those Laws. Those who think they are Untouchable in our system. – (Use your imagination.)

That's why society should spend more time investigating how living the Life of Attraction is much better than being governed by laws that can and will be broken, sooner or later. (But you be the judge of it.)

**The Law of Attraction, verses The Life of Attraction.**

Can you really tell the difference between a law controlling your existence, verses life in general causing you to be attracted to people and things naturally?

For example: People use a law to bond their relationship; (this is called, being married) and this changes the trajectory of a relationship altogether. The marriage-law is broken all the time (namely divorces, or even separation.) But people living the Life of Attraction instead of the Law of Attraction stay together longer without any law-controlling issues. So there's no law to be broken within their relationship.

When you feel people being attracted to you – you start improving yourself to have a better relationship with them. It's not a law making you feel this way; you are naturally drawing closer to that person because their inner-values are seen, heard, and felt by you. You're drawn to them by the way they express themselves to you. You see it within their eyes, smiles, and in the way they speak and act toward you.

And it's the same natural effect you get when someone is ready to (propose to you) as well. And any relationship is great; as long as it helps you be awaken, seeing the values within yourself, and the other person.

Stay awake! And see how the Life of Attraction is working for you non-stop. Release these comprehensions out amongst those you meet. Let others feel these awareness's coming from you. – Noticed yourself helping society improve socially and economically.

Since you are deeply Understanding how life works now; be reassured, there's more coming your way to change the way you look at things; and you're surely going to see a lot more about yourself changing naturally!

Just express true Wisdom and be Understandable! It's the best thing you'll ever do. – Don't let (worldly-information) trick or scare you away from these facts anymore!

You can tell if you are speaking Wisdom and Understanding versus speaking worldly information.

Here's how! ...When you're just saying things off the top of your mind, you'll giving information that leaves people guessing or assuming. – But when you speak wisdom and understanding you're causing people to know exactly what you expect from them. They will think and act according to discipline when they are with you. They will even remember you when you're not with them as well. – You will create a great-reminding affect upon their mind, no matter where they are. Because whenever they think of you, they are driven by the re-occurrence affect of being with you. 40

And every re-occurrence you have with someone you favor, is to be expected because you give the proof, evidence, and the feelings of being interested in them. – It's like watching them coming inside your lifestyle as a pieces of your life's puzzle.

Here's something to think about...

What good is it being human and don't know exactly what that means? Why be alive and not know the just of it all? What makes a person not want to know the true nature of their existence? Why would anyone not want to know why they're here on this planet? – It's for us to be fruitful, and multiply in all areas of life for future generations to come!

**A formula to successful living...**

If you apply the, who, what, when, where, why, and how affect to any situation, you'll have a much better success rate in any area of your life, with anyone.

Say for instance; you have someone in mind you want in your life today. The first thing to do is add the success formula to you and that person.

For instance…

Who - will this person be to me? And who will I, be to them?

What- can I give this person? And what can they give me?

When - can I be with this person? And when can they be with me?

Where - is this relationship headed? And where will this relationship be in the future?

Why - do I really want this person in my life? And why do they want me in their life?

How - do I really feel about this person? And how do they really feel about me?

This is how accurate you'll be when using this formula in any situation. This way, you're know the facts, and what to expect from a relationship with any person; even before the relationship begins. – You can see into the future if you really want to.

The main point is this; be sure your expectations are Similar to their expectations. – If you don't, then their expectations will overrule yours. (This is how failure is created.) Because sooner or later, you're going to offer a sacrifice you know you cannot afford to make – whether it's your time, money, or whatever. You'll feel your expectation losing ground with an expectation greater or lesser than your own.

On the other hand; if this success formula is flowing inside you naturally, you're be more at ease, relaxed, emotionally charge with great confident. You'll feel uplifted toward accomplishment, because you're in the process of receiving whatever you want without a doubt, from knowing the extent of your own efforts.

If you really want to see how the Life of Attraction works, and how it began – think about this, and put more thought into realizing this every day.                41

When you were conceived (or born); do you realize how amazing that moment was for you? You reach a point (the egg) that made it possible for you to be here today. There were millions of other (sperms-cells) racing alongside of you to find the (egg-opening) you discovered. – Out of all those little sperm-cells, you were the one going inside it.

– Just think of the odds of that moment?

Really think about this? – You could have easily missed that opening and fail wayside like the others. So doesn't this tell you how fortunate you are for being here today? If you really think about it, you'll feel yourself naturally being inside better living conditions. Being here right now, is proof and evident to that fact. You should feel how natural it is for you to live a better lifestyle; it's naturally embedded inside you.

So what's been keeping you from entering the lifestyle to prosperous living from the first day you were conceived? – Have you lost your way like many others have? Do you still see yourself living a life of wealth, health, and great prosperity today; because that's where you are headed and you know this is true.

And think about this while you are at it? And let this thought really sink in!

When you, and Millions of other sperm-cells were racing toward that egg, some of them got lost along the way – and maybe, when one of the others were at the entrance to that egg-opening; you nudged them aside, making your way inside-it instead. And that caused you to be inside this moment you're in (right now.)

This is brought to your attention because maybe, you should nudge your old ideas aside and come inside better living conditions right now. – (Just a thought!)

Right now; can you feel something inside you, making you want to open that entrance to better living conditions? Is something inside you, showing you the path to having more? Even now, aren't you more enlightened than you've ever been?

Realize this! – You are still on the same path when you were born. (It's a little difficult describing how to see that amazing moment of racing millions of other sperm-cells to the finish line that brought you here today.) And there is still so much more we can compare it to – so bare with me?

Doesn't this make you (feel certain) knowing you survived a challenge that was mainly impossible to others? You should never feel you're done searching for other openings in life. Just like you instinctively found the egg that gave you birth; these visions are showing you how to instinctively open doors to better opportunities for richer, happier, and prosperous living conditions.

– And always remember this: "Your Life is, an on-going process."

The author could have written entire books on any of these topics along. But (use your own imagination.) Or even write books about them yourself. There's plenty of room for more wisdom and understanding on how we could make better use of our time together here on earth, and get better results to our daily life.

**How to be prepared while attracting people to you...**

When your breath is fresh, people will be more inclined to talk to you up-close. – When your hair is well-groomed, people will compliment it. – When you dress nice and smell good, people breathe better around you. – When you have a business product or service that help people take care of their needs, they will want your product or services on a regular basis. – When you speak well about others, people will find you attractive and enjoy being with you. – When you speak kind words, kind words will return to you. – When you act with confidence, people will see you carrying your own weight. – When you smile, people will smile with you. – When you walk upright, people will see you knowing where you're going and naturally follow your leadership because you standout amongst other people.

These are only samples on how to make The Life of Attraction work. It depends on how much attention you give these attractions; and how you connect with the attractions of others. – It's like standing in front of a mirror seeing your own reflection, more or less.

Let's take a look at something else that will change the way you look at things from now on. – As you have seen, you've been asked certain questions during the reading of this book. And that's because, questions are your deepest power to revealing hidden secret in life, and for making newer discoveries.

And remember this, there are at least Ten answers to every One question.

So stay awake to these questions and feel them embracing your comprehensions with answers throughout these pages; and know that you're seeing how the Life of Attraction and Gravitational pulling sensations is working inside of life, through you.

And to add, you're also hearing lots of answers to questions you've had for a very long time, concerning attracting the opposite sex, making friends, gaining favors from almost everyone meet, everywhere you are. – Great progress is stacked in your favor now, so take more notice of this.

And remember; you never go anywhere. You're always in the here and now, because you never leave, You!

Also remember, there's going to be more divine wisdom such as this coming your way in the very near future from different people and different settings. And every time you want to make friends of any kind; Just remember, you won't get to know the real them, until they get to see and know the real You!

Okay, here's some questions for you:

If you had to guess which of two different characteristics to describe yourself with – which would you choose on average when walking throughout your day? And when you speak, what voice do you best say you use when talking to people in general?

A). Do you speak with a voice of <u>instructions</u>?

OR

B). Do you speak with a voice of <u>suggestions</u>?

Some of you may say, "It all depends on where I'm at, and who I'm with!" Not a good answer, because that doesn't answer the question. So don't let that limited response be your best answer because you are seeing a bigger picture of yourself.

Here's another question to go with the question above. –With everything you do all day?

A). Are you a person that says, I know?

OR

B). Are you a person that says, I believe?

These questions reveals the path you walk-on now, in the past, and will walk-on in the future if you really look at it. – So stay awake to these empowering questions from now on.

Start measuring, not judging your life; because sometimes you only experience certain stimulations fulfilling certain desires from time to time.

Because the truth is, you want to experience more "thrills and enlightenments" on a daily and regular basis, wouldn't you agree? Why just feel happiness from time to time, only for short periods of time, when you can be happy every day of your life?

**A story to enlighten you on seeing happiness every day.**

Here we go...

"There once was a Messiah that came to town on a regular basis, and everyone loved hearing what he had to say. When he got to town he begin asking questions concerning (God's) devotion. He asked the crowd of people listening to him – "If (God) asked you to make sacrifices for your fellowman, would you do it?" Everyone said, "Of course we would, without a doubt!" Then the Messiah asked, "If (God) asked you to die for him, would you?" Everyone replied, "Sure we would." Then the Messiah asked, "If (God) asked you to be happy every single day for the rest of your life, would you?" The Messiah watched everyone looking befuddled (lost and confused at that request.)

Now see yourself as one of those people standing in that crowd being asked those same questions right now.

Now, isn't' that something to think about?                                      44

Again, this book is going to help "Change the way you look at things, so the things you look at will change." *Dwight Dyer.*

Here's something mentioned earlier you should spend more time thinking about.

Remember when we say things like: "I went there. I'm going to this place and that place. I'm going over there." – We say a lot of things concerning going places, don't we?

But what if you found out you were wrong about those statements above? How would you feel about that?

"What do you mean?" you might ask; "How did you come to that conclusion? What sense are you trying to make? I don't quite understand that. And isn't it true when we say, we been there, and done that?"

Well, you are used to saying all those things mentioned above but haven't considered the true nature of them – not at all.

But the truth is; You have always been, here, inside you, no place else. You have never gone anywhere. – It's like feeling the universe revolving around you. If you really look closer at life and you in it, you'll feel yourself moving about inside it; not going anywhere.

Let me explain:

Now ask yourself, "Have I ever left, me – no matter where I'm at?"

You're always in the moment of now. – You, Are, Being in the place you are Right now! – Not going, nor ever gone anywhere!

When you start seeing yourself not leaving you; that's when you'll see exactly what this means, and you will feel yourself always active in the now – no place else! This is how you move away from laziness, procrastination, emptiness, and stand-still moments in life – no matter where you are, or who you're with.

Again, true wisdom and understanding works right now, not later after thinking about it. Because it makes you see clearly while giving insights you never thought existed, and you feel yourself breaking free from captivities that holds you back from truly seeing how life really work underneath it all; the way things happen inside you and others – even how your thoughts are changing right now while reading this book.

That's the nature and nurture of the Unseen controlling the Seen – or Scene of things.

And this book isn't about turning you into some sort of Religious person; it's about you taking a closer look at the unseen controlling the seen. But if you choose to look at it from a Religious point of view; then that's a decision you'll have to make, alone!

– This book is designed to help you take a deeper look inside you, not outside you – because everything you want, starts from believing within that you can have it!     45

Don't have opinions about life, have answers and let your awareness come forth from it (naturally) when you have (the insights) to see it with.

And remember, this book is planting new insights of growth inside you. Whether you give awareness to these insights of growth is up to you. If not, then happy-hunting finding these extraordinary visions elsewhere.

And if you hear of someone living better than you are; just remember, they are living these truths or something similar to them. It's them having full-awareness of these visions to true-living you're comprehending right now.

Here something else to think about...

You do have the power of insight and foresight, and here's how to see this...

Take a clock, and look closely at the second-hand going-around the face of it. Look at it for about a minute or two. – If you meditate on the second-hand going around the clock, you'll feel the speed in which the day is turning; also how everyone is living-by this movement each day. You will also feel how the day is turning into night, or vice versa. – Depending on the time of day. At the same time, you feel the power of "time" existing inside every living creature on the earth, no matter where they are.

If you see your life mainly about having more Time to give to others; (for instance, your family members or loved-ones.) Not just money and material things; but you'll feel yourself spending more time and effort communicating with them productively. – Now, that's real wealth to better living conditions.

What wisdom and understanding does, is keep you awake, implanting new discoveries inside your mind and heart every day, all day long.

And here's how it's doing that...

Just imagine feeling seeds being planted in good soil. (Wisdom and Understanding) are the good seeds; and you are the good soil. Now, imagine feeling these seeds taking root and sprouting (inside your awareness), making you feel awakened to a new person you're becoming; (leaving your old ways, to now, becoming a more enlightened person.)

That's what happens every time you read and absorb this book, you're being nourished with true Wisdom and Understanding to real living, so feel yourself sprouting like a beautiful flower, or an oak tree.

Here's another thought to consider ...

Did you know, that your desires create the things you're doing right now? The stronger your desire, the more compelled you are to moving toward it; and the results follow.

Keep this focus and you will feel the proof, evidence, and the results of everything you desire. Especially if you are desiring someone; because you are sending out vibrating signals toward that person (like a radio signal.)

With constant focus and meditation on your part (like someone fine-tuning) a radio station; that person is naturally affected by your intentions toward them; (good or bad.)

Even if you are the one receiving a signal from someone else, then their inner-signals are broadcasting to you, emotionally. You're the receiver from their signals of interest. – And if that person is not responding; be assured, they're getting your signals (or vice versa.) It could be mentally or just emotionally – but they do get your signals.

And if you, or they are not responding to these signals; then perhaps, neither of you are courageous enough nor confident to admit your interests to each other. This applies to any relationship you're trying to form with anyone. Again, you cannot relate to the real them, until they are able to relate to the real You!

There are no limits to how effective this vibrating-signal can have on people once you fully notice its effectiveness! And if someone comes to mind even though you weren't thinking about them; believe it or not, they are thinking about you. – It's the radio signals; or should we say, (it's the Life of Attraction) at work here.

We all know, that most leaders in society does not know how to teach or give real living knowledge to the whole of humankind. Maybe they do know, but won't take the time to teach it to everyone. Or, they are just keeping it for themselves, for unknown reasons.

But as long as you stay involved with wisdom and understanding that can and will work for you on a daily basis, it won't matter if society is only living by information, alone. – So "LIVE Your Life to the Fullest!" Have more of Everything you want, and don't be afraid to have it! – It's your Right! But be careful and disciplined with this truth, don't over think it.

Here's an image to remember:

Imagine seeing logs floating, just drifting along the current headed downstream in one direction. Now think of yourself being one of those logs drifting like it's headed nowhere in particular.

If you're not living the life you want to live, then see yourself drifting with no destination, and (measure) yourself drifting with no specific purpose in this time of being.

With this concept resonating in your mind, recalibrate your life and make a stand. Pull yourself out of any moment you do not enjoy being in! You must let wisdom and understanding show you how to have More money, power, friendships, opportunities, lovers, loved-ones, and so much more. You want this great power and influence; don't you?

**Measuring yourself to everyone and everything in life.**

Life is much better when you're measuring yourself to things, instead of judging them. If you look at your life like a measuring stick, sort of speaking, you'll know exactly how close you're getting to something you want – even if it's with certain people, because you're the one determining how much time and effort you want to give them.

If you make a judgment toward someone, you're making a (guess-you-made-it-opinion) with that judgment. That part of you judging things is the reason you're not attaching yourself to it; and it's harder connecting with someone when trying to make a less (valuable) claim for them. Just remember; Judging keeps you disconnected!

But when you measure yourself to someone or something, you're more in control of the income and outcome of things; simply because you can feel your efforts and the effects you have with it. You know how much is leaving you verses how much is coming back to you. – You feel the effects of whatever you say and do with anyone you meet. You know exactly how much you (want to keep) or (give away) because you notice and feel the energy coming and going away from you.

Measuring, is a binary or (eliminating process) naturally embedded inside you, and it's activated as soon as you make contact with someone or some things. It helps you know exactly when you are gaining momentum or losing ground with your endeavors. – You mainly call it (if this is the case) your gut feeling, or instincts warning you ahead of time. That's how you keep a close watch on the things coming and going from your life.

**Can you see things happen before they occur?**

You're always using your measuring skills anyway, with mostly everything you do. For instance when you feel tired or sleepy, when you are hungry or thirsty, and with any other desirable appetite you have concerning human nature. This is how you determine if and when you have enough, or not had enough of something.

And it's also how you are measuring your beliefs from the way you feel while reading this book, trying to determine how real these visions are to you. You have always been craving to have this kind of wisdom and understanding inside you, but didn't know to what extent you were craving it for, (If this is the case.)

At this point, you are sure you've made a discovery with what's been missing in your life. And by waking-up to your measuring skills within, you see newer possibilities, more than you ever have before. Because life is becoming much clearer while learning these secrets to better living conditions. Now you know exactly what's going to happen in your life while applying these visions to your efforts; and they will assist you from now on.

Here's a thought...

Let's assume you're interested in someone, which everyone does. 48

The first thing you want to do, is make them feel relaxed with your efforts toward them. Speak and act according to the way you want them to treat you. (But reverse this effect onto them.) As the old saying goes; "Treat others as you would like to be treated."

Because, when you measure your expectations to someone else; it's either being accepted, or rejected with a losing ground feeling; (and you don't want this to ever happen.) Once you start an interaction with someone, they are depending on you to carry most of the interactions with them. Again, you started this interaction, so take the lead and keep their intended reaction on high, and this makes the relationship stronger.

Moving on to a more enlightened concept from the above...

Let's look at this from another angle...

Your mind is capable of creating Holograms, or Hallucinations.

A hologram is an image of something or someone you want to come into reality. It's an image within your imagination. A hallucination is something fantasized about as being an illusion, a mirage, a delusion, or even a nightmare.

And by imagining having something so strongly – whether it's a person or whatever, you create a holographic image in your mind. But if you're not following through and acting upon that holographic image it can turn-out only being a hallucination. It all depends on the energy you create for that holographic image, or the lack-of it.

A hologram stays with you, while a hallucination slowly fades-away after you're done exploring the possibility of it. Like dreams, they basically enter your mind while sleeping as a form of a hallucination, or nightmare. (Even though, you wish some dream were real!)

A hologram (an imaginary image) is the first stage for creating something into reality, verses something never becoming a reality at all, (in other words, you are hallucinating.) Because when you measure what you believe with what you assume; your feelings, emotions, and instincts together starts working harder at grasping the sense of things.

And if you're not able to measure the difference between a hologram or hallucination, then you're emotionally drifting without making anything concrete. This causes a mental hallucination, because the hologram never becomes a reality.

And you'll know if something is real to you, because of the way you behave toward it. You simply feel that interest giving you a certain focus; the proof is in the pudding sort of speaking. A bond is naturally created from the connection you have with something real.

**How to turn a holographic image of a relationship into reality.**

When you're with someone you enjoy and trying to build a relationship with them, pay attention to the way you look at each other, the way you speak to each other, and the way you touch each other, mentally, emotionally, and even physically.                49

– Notice how you feel toward them, and they toward you. Observe the smile of gratitude they give you. And if you really look at them, you'll see that they are really bringing a holographic image of you to life as well.

This measuring skill is used in your work areas, friendships, business, or whatever. People just want to know if what you say and do is real – not something sugar-coated to create hallucinations in their mind. They want to trust who you are through their feelings. – So live like you're not-only being seen or heard, but also felt! – Embrace the proof, evidence, and the results from whatever you say or do, no matter where you are!

While you're reading (sitting or standing) right now, feel these insights coming from these pages enlightening your comprehensions as they are describing the holographic image of a brighter future for you.

And when you put this book down and go back to those daily routines of the past, most of these insights will probably fade and become (a hallucination.) Those old thoughts of yours will try to remove what's being shown in these pages to put you back in that mindset you used to serve, because your old ways of thinking won't give-up so easily.

But, every time you read, or re-read this book, it removes your old thoughts and replace them with newer ones!

There are things inside of life you haven't begun to start seeing, or realizing; because society's leaders hasn't developed the courage to show, nor express the true nature of what's (hidden) in our mist going unnoticed every day.

But be assured; you won't have to be concerned about it, as long as you keep these visions turned-on inside your awareness, no matter what else happens around you. There will always be a (mental reminder) asking you to pick this book-up and absorb these pages so you can stay in the mindset of seeing better things coming your way. – Reading this book on a regular basis helps you see all negative thoughts and feelings in and around you. Also, these visions keeps you away from the negative side of life. Even if you seem uncertain, or just out of sync; a Mental voice from your subconscious will express itself, reminding you to keep a close watch on your brighter future, today.

And remember, you're seeing how to take better steps creating the path you want to having a brighter future each day, because you're absorbing "More visions" and nothing can remove them, but you!

Now let's spend more time on the question asked earlier concerning how you speak on average each day.

Here's the question again, but paraphrased this time...

When you speak; Do you speak with a voice of Instructions, or a voice of Suggestions?

The reason you are asked this question is because, during your entire lifetime you're either going to be teaching or telling someone something. And there is a big difference between the two.

When you're teaching someone something, basically you're instructing them. But when you're telling someone something, you're only giving them suggestions. –People learn "more" when you have their full attention. You enlighten and capture their mind like flipping-on a switch. They enjoy listening to you, and this makes them feel they are measuring you from their feelings; and it becomes an Attraction.

Can't you see how people react when you speak to them? Do they get involved in your conversation; or do they stand there listening, trying to make sense out of something you're saying? And if they do respond, does it seem they're giving you their suggestions in return?

Just watch closely how people act when you're talking without instruction, you'll observe others listening and filling their mind with suggestions about you. And when you observe someone else speaking without instructions, you're doing the same thing, filling your mind with suggestions about them. –So speak with instructions and people will naturally follow along with you, more than they would if you are only giving them suggestions.

**Reaching a point where there is "No return."**

What you're discovering while reading this book is – you're not going to return to that old lifestyle you once served.

Just think of it this way!… Since you have come this far, you're going to finish this book because it's the same comparison of taking a balloon out of its rapper, blowing it up, and trying to place-it-back inside the same rapper it came out of – you can't do it!

Unless you release the air from it. – But why would you do that?

Well, the same applies to returning to your old lifestyle after absorbing these amazing visions and insights, because your comprehensions are getting bigger and expanding beyond that boundary now. – You just can't live like that anymore!

Your mind has become so enlightened, that it's going way-beyond the way you used to see things in the past. It's being filled with newer-awareness' of yourself, other people, and life in general.

Now you will feel better knowing you have Instructions, Disciplines, and Corrections showing you a better way of living to the fullest. And imagine what it's going to feel-like when people hear you applying your awareness of things to their conversations. Your voice will be that of a conductor, teacher, and leader, expressing itself inside the ears of your listeners like you're teaching them something important with every word you speak. You will communicate more effectively with them, (and vice versa.)                51

You'll see most people thinking while speaking with you; "Now, that's, something I wanted to hear you say to me!" You'll see it in their eyes, and upon their face.

Isn't this better knowing you're a person giving instructions, mainly? I mean, look at what's happening to you while reading the instructions, disciplines, and corrections in this book. – Doesn't it seem like you are personally hearing the voices of wisdom and understanding now?

You can imagine how people will feel hearing you instructing them to learn something new, verses giving them suggestions? They'll feel much better knowing you are giving them something to really think about; You!

Before going any further, answer this question: Are you afraid of real success?

We're not talking about the success of the world. But true Success. The Success of (You) where success begins, and ends. – With YOU!

The question again is, Are you afraid of being the person you are meant to be, living the life you are meant to live; having favor with everyone that comes in contact with you?

And if you have doubts of being this person; don't be! Because deep down inside; you are a great person, a wise teacher, a good counselor, a great role-model, etc. – Just look closely when you're showing others how, when, and what to do sometimes. You are a natural born leader if you really looked back at your life and see that up to now.

You've always walked a path that shows what is, and what will be – not just, what was.

Do you see how you've always been living with this leadership skill in the past? And leaders always find their way; they see the secret path into a world of many possibilities.

People with (Leadership skills) see the Proof, Evidence, and Results from whatever they say and do.

Do you see these visions showing you how to opening that hidden dimensional world of progress in your mist, the world of the unseen controlling the scene of things around you? Do you feel this (egg-opening) now? The one identical to the opening when you were conceived?

"Yes. A little," you might say.

Now prepare yourself; you're going inside a world where most people do not see the unseen controlling the scene of things.

Does the word, "Microscopic" ring a bell? There's a whole world existing hidden from the naked-eye. Things never seen because of not considering they are there. And because of being closed minded, a lot of things escape most people's awareness of them. And inside this hidden world is where a lot of unanswered questions, and possibilities still remain.                                                                 52

There are places on earth mankind still haven't discovered yet; also places outside our hemisphere that hasn't been visited either. And yet, we want questions answered no matter how long it takes or who has to be sacrificed to achieve those discoveries.

Let me explain it another way.

We live in a 2-dimensional and 3-dimensional world of things. One is on the surface, underneath the surface, and in-between the unseen controlling the scene of things. (Or should we say) the Spiritual world. – Mainly, that's how we explore the true nature of existence, and each other.

Inside each of us is an unknown universe of ideas and behaviors (good or bad.) They are hidden within us until we have causes or reasons to reveal them to others.

This is brought to your attention because it's going to help you see deeper inside your life and the world around you. You are going to define a better relationship with anyone you choose; plus improve the way you look at people in general.

Now with that said:

Remember having a dream that don't make sense? You woke-up wondering why you had a dream such as that! While you were asleep those hidden life-forms in the unseen world are aware that you're not awake to stop them from invading your mind.

Now stay with me – the point will be made.

You remember having that dream, and know it couldn't been you in it! But still, you felt you were living the experience of that dream. You woke-up regretting that dream, unless it was a happy dream! – You felt like something-else was using you (like a puppet) while you were asleep. It was like something unknown to you was trying to express itself through you. Or like something-else trying to come to reality through you.

Basically; it's those unseen forces that's been using you like a puppet to play-out their existence. This is how they express their existence because they can't take human form. – And it's the same when you're displaying a lifestyle you don't enjoy living.

Case in point – you are doing the same thing every time you act or answer to someone else's lifestyle. You are not living or acting according to your own. You're being treated like a puppet on a sting doing what you are made, or told to do without realizing it.

Since you (if this is the case) are mostly living a lifestyle of someone else, you aren't fully aware of your own existence, not using your comprehensions to the fullest, nor aware of how wonderful you really are – outside forces and conditions are taking-over (using you like a puppet); especially when you're thinking and feeling unappreciated, nor appearing productive. That's the best opportunity for outside forces to tie their stings (or conditions) to your behaviors. – And this happens every time you show you don't have a clue, or a grip on your own lifestyle.                                                     53

**On the subject of regrets...**

Look back in your past, at something you said or did with regret? – And ask yourself; "What could I have said or done (to that situation) that would've made it work out better for me?"

– What would you change if you could go back and do something over again, right now? – And if you make this a steady practice seeing how to put a (second chance) in place before you need one – then you'll be able to turn your life in any direction you choose. You'll be able to put your lifestyle on the course you intended it to be in the first place, without regrets. You will see a clearer pathway to better living conditions presenting itself to you. – And remember: It's only your lifestyle that comes and goes, while you are always being in the moment of, right now – no matter what time of day it is, or who you are with.

That simple awareness of knowing how to put a (second chance) in place before you need one, has more power and punch to it than you can imagine, once you apply it to all your situations! –You see how easier it is turning your life around; having fewer regrets in your life now.

With that resonating in your mind right now – can't you see (if this is the case) how you've been treated like a puppet on a string without being aware of it? Just look at your whole lifestyle and see if this is true or not?

Many followers in the world today, believe humankind is headed to an end. But that's not true. We are still in the early stage of our existence, and now starting to understand our real journey into richer and prosperous living conditions for all of humankind.

For instance – start keeping an eye on people becoming rich every day? You'll see how life is spreading its wealth around the world to so many people. It might seem slow to some people; but there's so much evidence showing people becoming richer every single day, and a time is coming when everyone will enjoy a very enriching lifestyle. And, (if this is the case) you don't choose to have a fair-share of this wealth during your lifetime, then your children or their children will receive it.

Here's a way to keep a close watch on this fact. – Once a day, check the status of people becoming rich. You can do this each week, or monthly if you choose; even every year. (Use your imagination.) – Don't just take the author's word.

The status of rich people according to worldsrichpeople.com and web-page-finance.com there are now 2170-Billionaires and 12-million Millionaires on the planet. (Record count for 8-14-2015.) – This is proof from a recent research!

The author remembers when, in the late 70s and early 80s, there were 100-Billionaires and 2.2 million-Millionaires on the planet. A great leap from about 35-years ago.

Just imagine what the next 35-years will look like concerning the status of rich people? And you can easily be the next Millionaire, if only you truly believe it! – This is Paradise forming on our planet steadily without most people's awareness of it.

There's is so much more for us to learn and do concerning prosperous living conditions, that we are just beginning our venture into the world of the unknown to living happier, healthier and richer than we can imagine. – Sooner or later, it's going to reach all of humankind. And believe this, true wealth and riches will come your way when you truly open-up to it.

– Again, it's how you interpret a rich lifestyle – and yourself with it.

Wisdom and Understanding has more work to be done, and so do we. Just knowing each of us has a lot missing from our awareness concerning togetherness with those around us; that's why we are tried and tested each day, to see if we're getting the whole message to the bigger picture, together – and we haven't, not yet. But we will!

**Using your imagination.**

– Aren't there people you want to be with, things you want to have, places you want to be, and a lifestyle you want to live? – Well, just act like you want these things to occur!

Each of us have dreams, goals, and plan to live a better lifestyle. But most people are still wondering how to do that exactly, that they've implanted deep inside their minds, holograms or even hallucinations throughout the years. This has caused faint-visions or dull-images of a brighter future – like living in big beautiful homes, driving brand new cars, filling their pockets, purses, or bank-accounts with large sums of money, being with people they desire, or just wearing clothes that describe their best qualities in this very moment in time.

**Holograms can turn out being Hallucinations**.

Are you living, manifesting your life from holograms – or from some hallucination that you hope will turn into a reality?

Do you see yourself living in a big beautiful home, driving brand-new vehicles, wearing clothing that best describe your greatest qualities, having a fun-filled lifestyle, everyday?

Because when picturing something you really want in life; At first, you put a (holographic picture) in your mind filled with hope and possibility. But if weak-actions are put in play on your part, those images begin fading, becoming a fantasy from wishful thinking. In the end, becomes a failed attempt – a hallucination.

A hallucination (or fantasy) can best be described by the way you pursue someone or some things only from intentions, instead of with much effort on your part. – The old saying goes; "Faith without work, is dead! –If first, you don't succeed; try and try, again!" and many others clichés you can think of.                                                55

Some people spend their entire lives letting holograms turn into hallucinations from how they envision things to be. They have imprinted an hallucination so deeply inside their imagination that they are basically living by assumptions, guessing their way through life with many things they say and do.

Telling themselves, they want some things so badly that they can taste it! But when it comes to acknowledging the sacrifices and consequences that comes with that desire, they refuse to stay focused for it. They are so possessive from wanting it to be true, that they've misread so many signals on how to truly obtain it. – And people do this all the time in new relationships of all kinds.

Let's look even deeper at this fact:

(If this the case.) Remember when someone breaks a promise you wanted them to keep; (such as a date), personal or business? You immediately peek inside your imagination (or should we say) inside the world of the unseen, trying to envision every possibility of (what might be) with that person.

You create holographic images of having good-times with that person. And you envision all kinds of thoughts, even feelings for that person. All from a holographic mindset which sometimes end-up being a hallucination. Because when time came for the date, they never called or showed up. (And there are other factors causing that person to delay meeting with you.) This makes those holographic images you have for that person fade-away. You start thinking thoughts like; "Why did they stand-me-up? What did I do wrong? Was it me?"

Then the questioning part of your mind begins removing that holographic image of that person. – Now you're in a state of hallucination because your mind drift in and out of what might-have-been. The mental fabric of your mind becomes uncomfortable and begins removing the images of that person out of your thoughts.

**Does manifesting really work?** – Yes it does!

Here's a test to prove manifesting can really work. For instance, a new relationship.

The next time you are just standing around waiting for whatever reasons, and someone attractive comes and stands close to you. – First, take a close look at them; then say with passion; "You know, I've imagined meeting someone exactly like you for quite some time now. – But the face I had in mind, wasn't very clear, until now. – What's your name?"

Watch the smile rise upon their face; you'll notice yourself seeing eye-to-eye, thinking like-minded with that person because you've made a holographic impression of meeting someone like them that it becomes a reality, and a new relationship is born. And it's only an ice-breaker. You can create others! – And remember, it's in the way you deliver your message to (Male or Female.)                                    56

Can you see the image on that person's face behind that great compliment you will give them? Whatever they were thinking before you say that, won't matter as much, because you're making them feel appreciated. And a compliment given at the right time and right way, will change the trajectory of anyone's mind, and heart.

And if you look deeper inside your imagination, you'll see other similar compliments to give them and keep their interests. They won't be able to resist being with you. You're doing something different than others and that makes that person feel attracted to you (or vice versa.) – And maybe, you're the person they've imagined meeting as well.

Again, what you're searching for, is also searching for you. – And remember, everything is a hologram until you physically turn it into a reality. So don't let your hologram turn into a hallucination. Make more contact with people around you from your holographic point of view; and avoid wishful thinking, hoping things will come true!

There is so much more to say about any one of these topics, and if you're looking for a topic for your own book – then these visions have shown you many topics to start with.

When true Wisdom and Understanding strikes; you feel its affects right then, and it's undeniable! (It's like striking a hammer to iron) and the blade becomes noticeable; just like these visions are striking your comprehensions, and your awareness to better living conditions is becoming more noticeable right now.

You are noticing your comprehensions being filled with wisdom and understanding, and you'll starting to feel darkness and negativity leaving your thoughts naturally. They hide in two-places – deep inside the mind, and deep inside the heart. Hidden from people's awareness of them. – Most people won't look there. Darkness cannot live inside these lights, and you're not a shadow keeper any more.

So keep these lights-on inside your awareness. Stay in the analyzing awaken state of being wiser and understandable at all times and move toward your true destiny, laying down a clear pathway to enriching your lifestyle for future generations to come.

A wise person will leave an inheritance (if this is the case) for their children's children.

An inheritance is built by wisdom and understanding you can passed-on-to generations to come. Those generations following will have a much easier lifestyle, free from faults and misfortunes left behind to endure from past generations.

Books like this will show you and future generations coming how to live a much easier life, filled with great happiness and togetherness. If you look back many years ago, (In history books) you'll see your forefathers and mothers didn't have true wisdom and understanding ready made available for them like you do now. It's time to have a better lifestyle instead of being compliant to the-old-one. Let's put better living conditions in place for everyone – including the poor and less fortunate.

Society is too separate from each other to stay on the path its on. We have newer ways of coming together as a whole community now, not living in special groups anymore. – Selfish living is old, and outdated. That's what's holding society back.

The computer age is proof we're able to communicate with anyone around the world at the touch of a button. – We all want healthier communities providing us with things to prosper into a newer age of living, like the new age of computers growing stronger every day. We must keep up together so we can manage and endure things we haven't seen or considered yet.

There's a lot coming concerning (more people on the planet, future children with their issues and ideals, education on all levels, computers, crimes, and a lot more) we haven't seen yet – And you can bank on that!

As said before, in the beginning of this book: It isn't written to coach you into monetary values. Well, not indirectly, even though you will sometimes feel it giving instructions for creating monetary values through slip-streams of your awareness at any given moment.

And here's one of those giving moments.

One way to view the world of money is through its values. It's here for your desires, wants, and even to fulfill certain cravings you have. (And you know what I mean!)

Money flows throughout the system like water, electricity, and even energy, providing you the lifestyle you already live. But the thing of it is, money has limits, and so do you, no matter what you think.

One way to view the (lack of money) is like seeing birds flying overhead out of reach keeping their distance like they're not interested in you. – And every time you run-out of it (if this is the case), it's like watching money fly away as fast as you get it. – This is a description for those choosing to be poor, or feeling less fortunate!

There are so many ways people view money and its values. – Some people say: "I just want money to pay bills, and maybe take a vacation; at least, once a year." or "I want money to help those less fortunate." or "I just want money to have fun with." or "Money is the root of all evil!" But still, everyone have many reasons and purpose to spend their entire lives creating way to have it!

So then; how does one find the balancing-act concerning, having more money?

Look at what money does and how it affects your way of living. (If this is the case); Do you struggle to make ends meet every day, every week, every month – and it has been this way for you a great number of years; And still is? – Stop letting this happen to you?!

Then you might say; "But, how? How can I just let go of the things I've been working hard to keep every day? – I'm so used to doing what I always do every day, weekly, each month, and year-round!"

It's not really about the things you are used to doing. – It's about (not doing) the things you could be doing for the rest of your life; like building and living a more productive enriching lifestyle for you and future generations to come, starting from where you are right now!

**Can you see into the future?**

Do you ever hear people speaking about seeing into the future? This might sound like some sort of prediction here; And it is! – It's something you do anyway, and don't know you're doing it. – But you will, once you take a closer look at it.

Don't you know what time to be at your job, or an appointment? Don't you know what clothes you are going to wear to your next place of visit? You know when you are going to bed. Even you know, what time you're going to be with certain people each day. – Etcetera, etcetera, etcetera. (Use your imagination.)

Now to add to that question: – **Can you see into your own future?**

Yes you can. But you might feel a little uncertain, because you might not have someone to talk about it.

– And what do you think, planning something is? – It's seeing into the future. When you write down your ideas, or constantly see images (or holograms) of yourself doing things you want done – you are seeing into the future. – When you're taking a bath or shower, grooming yourself, getting dressed, or whatever. Don't you basically know how you're going to look, even before you get started with these preparations?

Whenever you start doing anything, your holograms has already started developing in your mind way-before you even consider getting involved with it. That's why your body is always behind any activity, trying to catchup to those images already laid-out within your mind.

Do you see where this is going now?

That's right, you're becoming more aware of seeing yourself creating your own future.

And to add: Your passion is delayed from some holograms because you don't feel the joy of whatever you're imagining at the time. But with steady focus and desire you'll eventually start applying yourself to those holographic images and catch-up to them with your reality actions.

And here's a thought...

Remember when you're going for a ride in a vehicle and feel it carrying you to your destination? Well, the same happens every time you feel your inner-strength making you do some-things naturally.

– When you are preparing for a job interview, or an amazing date with someone; aren't you envisioning how it will turn-out before it does? When you go to any store to get what you want; aren't you measuring the value of your dollars before making any purchase you want?

And if you set an appointment for any reason, today, next week, a month, or even a year from now, you will have set in motion the outcome of things for your future. You're developing the exactly nature of knowing what's going to happen before it does.

It's your inner-feelings joined with life, picking you up, molding your awareness turning it into actions, then pointing your mentality in a direction that puts your energy to use and make accomplishments happen, naturally.

Just broaden your awareness of seeing how you are making things happen today and apply the same comprehensions to your future – that's all.

You are seeing how to stop losing ground, standing still in those situations you once lived in the past, because you have the visions and steps to have a brighter future.

You should also know that there's going to be "More" books such as this, coming your way in the future. – Do you see yourself reading More books like this in the future? – Don't you know you're going to launch a product or service into the world successfully, someday?

Do you imagine driving and owning vehicles of your dream, someday? Do you see yourself living in your dream home, and owning a big business someday? Do you see yourself inside banks standing in front of tellers, depositing or withdrawing large-sums of money for you and your loved-ones?

Even the author sees Thousands, and even Millions of people using this book, turning their lives around in the very near future as it travels through the different channels that are being set in motion for it. He see himself doing television shows with live audiences, radio talk-shows, published in High-quality magazine articles, the news, and even signing autographs in many cities and states – also in different countries once this book is translated in other languages.

Can you see him doing these things in the future as well? (Yes you can.)

These are holograms of the future, preparing to be manifested into reality.

And the question still remains: "Can (You) see into (your own future now?)"

Here something else to see unfolding before your very eyes! – Are you aware, when you're stressing or struggling to keep up with certain situations, you are fluctuating going in and out, up and down with your mind and emotions, watching your living conditions (if this is the case) being unstable from the things you say and do, sometimes?

Can't you see ahead of time, that children today are bringing a whole-new-set of rules, regulations, and conditions to a whole new lifestyle with different kinds of people in the future? Today, technology is causing children to have different views and values with discipline, instructions, and corrections.

Some people find it more challenging to solve problems children are faced with today. And some of their issues have challenges that require solutions parents have no clue of, because of the changing of times, and what it's bringing with it. – Like the computer age.

Just like our fore-mothers and forefathers missed-out-on a lot of things from not keeping up with the changing of time, nor having wisdom and understanding at their disposal. –

(Only, if they could see us now!)

Just look at the educational system for one-thing? – Some of it seems like a whole new language to learn. – Education is changing so fast, that it's challenging for a lot of people to keep-up; and it seems like some-things are preparing to leave a lot of people behind.

Every day, someone complains about situations they cannot relate too, because of not seeing what's taking place for the future. And each of us is experiencing a lifetime filled with much abundance, but not everyone sees this, from a lack of clearly interpreting the things going on around them.

Now when you clearly interpret things going on around you now, you'll also clearly see things taking place in the future as you move forward with your endeavors. You'll be ahead of the game, sort of speaking.

– Take a good look at society, and you'll see most people not using these visions at all; every gender (young and old.) – Go ahead, take a closer look at everyone, everywhere?

You are a fixer of life now, because you have the inner-ability to create and solve any problem in your life. This doesn't require you having faith or believing-in anything. Just know, you are a purpose for being human with the will-power to make whatever you want happen, and start doing it now!

Here's a programming you can practice doing naturally, just for the fun of it.

The reality you create within, is the same reality that will naturally be place in the world around you. – You should feel this happening inside your world all the time.

–By living inside the reflection of a lifestyle you see yourself in, you'll be taking action toward the things you truly want to happen. Don't think of attempting to have it! – Just do it! – Get mentally and emotionally involved with the lifestyle you see yourself in. This will naturally make you act upon it! – And this way, you'll make living more enjoyable.

Do you remember the last time, you really enjoyed having a fun-filled day? Go back and retrieve that same mindset. Start thinking and feeling those same thoughts and actions you felt then, right now! Put that wonderful lifestyle back in place, now; and you'll begin experiencing the life you truly want to live – and also have control of it.

Concentrate on that energy and never let it escape your awareness again. – Hold-on to that which really works for you. And everyone knows, that (when you are happy) that's when you cannot-only feel it, but you're naturally holding the magic hidden inside of life.

...(Happiness is something everyone craves to have!)...

Have you ever heard someone say, rich people have a different mindset than others?

Well. That's true, because they see things from a more enlightened point of view.

Most people relax or have fun only on weekends; not during the course of the week. Weekends are their priority for relaxing and having fun while rich people do it every single day, throughout each year.

Some people only enjoy the Weekend because of time restrains, from jobs, obligations, responsibilities, or promises (Use your imagination) knowing those unfinished tasks are waiting for them to return and finish them every week. They measure their fun and relaxation by the freedom given to them, not created by them.

Like Friday's, because that's a day they can relax after a long week of traveling back and forth to work, and other obligations. They can finally get out of the rat-race, sort of speaking and take their earnings and measure out a course of fun and relaxation with those they care about.

Then there is Saturday, where people spend more time with family-members, friends, or side interests they have; or just have fun with no worries or pressure of being anywhere on that day unless work or responsibility is still required of them.

Now on Sunday, some people use this day to get more rest, fulfill spiritual interests, and prepare for weekly challenges ahead of them. But for the rest of the week, most of their weekend interests are forgotten or put aside because of not being part of their weekly norms. And this living pattern is repeated every week, monthly, throughout each year.

This lifestyle is repeated so much! – No wonder the system is like it is. And the (Powers to Be) is very aware of society's repeated behaviors.

Rich people see ways for traveling a whole new path to living. – They see every day as a fun-filled or relaxing day, if that's what they want it to be. They treat any day as a day of rest, relaxation, or whatever. They do things from a more accurate point of view and don't assume anything. They spend most of their time investing, making sure their time and energy is spent wisely, not wasted.

They see things on their terms; managing progress instead of letting progress manage them. – That's why, they think differently from other people.

So do as rich people do. Greet each day as a day of rest and relaxation. And if you want wealth and riches, start managing your progress instead of letting progress manage you – that's a sure way of having a fun-filled lifestyle. It's just a matter of changing the way you look at things, then the things you look at will change.

**How to make manifestation work and feel it coming into reality.**

You have to feel something stabilizing itself, in order to know if it's becoming a reality.

Here's an example...Think of a vehicle you want to drive right now. (And really use your senses, and your imagination.)

"...Now feel... yourself opening the door getting into that vehicle, sitting in it smelling that new interior smell, adjusting your seat, adjusting the mirrors, putting your seatbelt on – now sticking the key in the ignition listening to the engine running, putting your foot on the brakes changing gears, checking traffic and pulling away from that parking spot you are in."

Take it for a test-drive to a grocery store, or wherever? The more you tune-in-to this hologram, the realer it becomes. Feel yourself picturing this action taking place in your lifestyle, right now. – This is what it mean by manifesting something into reality.

Stop reading for a minute and feel this hologram? Get the full details of it. And make sure your holographic images don't turn into a hallucination.

Now. No matter what other vehicle you get in, you will instinctively feel this holographic images in your mindset. It's going to magnetically enhance your chances for receiving that vehicle. – You are seeing and feeling into the future my friend.

And you can do this with anything or anyone, any time you choose.

See into your future.

– But don't just see it..."feel...inside it." Use your body-mind and senses to measure your course of actions by feelings inside this powerful technique. Stay inside this mindset, no matter what else you do!

Some of you might feel that this is a bit much for an outcome. But let's be honest? What else has worked for you in the past concerning bringing something into reality; making something happen the way you want it?

Give it a try – you have nothing to lose! – Let's just have some fun together. Don't worry, it's just you and me. – "I really believe-in you."

Take time-out each day doing this fun fulfilling activity.

Put the book down when you start joining your life to reality on this level, because it matters when you're harnessing and holding your imagination. And remember, your success only happens when you measure yourself to it!

Now, let's do a personal make-over for yourself; shall we?

If you wanted to be the person you've always imagined being...How would your hairstyle look? Make it very attractive.

Now "hold... that vision" and don't let go of it!

How does your face look? Now "hold ...that facial look!"

How does your body look? Now imagine, and "feel... that vision."

How much do you want to weigh? "Feel... yourself, holding... that weight," and don't let go of it! – Hold these images inside your imagination every day; and don't let go until they become your reality! – Even little hints of visions will do just fine! Because they will grow with time and effort.

How does your soul-mate(s) look? Look into their eyes, see them smiling at you. – Now look at their hair for (color and length), their face (all over), their neck, shoulders, arms, (skin-color and tone), chest or breasts (size and shape), waist-line (size), hips (curves), thighs, legs (length and firmness), and their feet.

"Hold... and... Feel" their presence, every part of them with your imagination. "Touch them with your feelings and emotions."

See the hologram of that person standing before you, smiling and loving you like no one else ever have? – And you definitely want this to happen! Now "hold..." these thoughts of that person, and don't let go!

And remember, if you need help creating images of any kind; there are lots of books, magazines, or whatever, out there to assist you. (Use your imagination.)

Also create the homes, lifestyle, or clothing you want to wear the same way you do with other holographic programming. – Be open-minded.

Now. How much money do you want in your pocket, purse, or billfold right now? Think of a number, then "feel... yourself reaching in your pocket, purse, or billfold taking it out, counting it," and ready to do whatever you want with it.

"Hold... these feeling" and don't let go!

The more you do these fun-time exercises, the more capable your holograms will come true. – Also remember: You are changing the way you look at things so the things you look at will change for you.

So with all these expectations resonating inside your mind, never go back to the way you were living (if this is the case) standing alone, walking by yourself, thinking selfishly, or sitting apart from others, treating them like they're not part of your expectations.

People need you, and you need them. – It's "People Wealth." So stop being selfish and naïve to this fact.

If there was one thing to hear life saying to us; it would be, "Everyone must learn to treat each other the way they want to be treated. They should care for each other in ways they can't begin to imagine!"

– Can't you hear life saying that to?

With these insights developing inside you; are you going to accept this new lifestyle you have finally discovered, or go back to a lifestyle that denied you real living (if this is the case?)

With these visions, and others coming; you'll soon see More of everything coming your way – because life is not only showing you how to have More, but it's also giving you More to give others at the same time, including, learning how to have more money.

And the system is filled with "Money" flowing everywhere inside it. Some people call it (Loop-holes or Slip-streams) such as (SSI Social Security Income, Unemployment benefits, Government aid programs of all kinds, Lotteries of all kinds, and Game-show giveaways); and there are many others you know of yourself. (Use your imagination.)

And some people don't work for a living at all. And yet, they still live very productive lifestyles! – Are you still enjoying this down-pour coming inside your awareness?

Here's a description for keeping up with money, if you want "More" of it.

Money, is like seeing race-cars going around a race-track at a hundred-miles per-hour; you must keep your eyes on every car at every turn, (or should we say) you must keep a close eye on every dollar you spend. – And if you want great sums-of-money; put yourself in the driver-seat, or (seat of millionaires.) You'll have a better idea on how fast money comes and goes around in your lifestyle. Just be ready to make decisions like rich people do, at the right time.

Because everything else you do, is like watching race-car passing-by (or should we say), watching the lifestyle of rich people passing by you. – All you have to remember is this, Money is always moving fast in the system; even through your hands. Just notice how you're making decisions with the money you have. So stop acting like you are sitting in the stand watching other people become richer! – Get inside this lifestyle; don't sit or stand around watching other people become rich. – Do it yourself! It's where you truly belong. Or you'll see yourself cheering for someone else's rich lifestyle and won't have one of your-own.                                          65

A lot of people think life's simple tasks are hard to achieve, and that's why you hear them say; "It's easier said, than done!" about making accomplishments.

No, it's, not!

– And successful people say; "Actions speak louder than word?" Because rich lifestyles are built when you start creating it; not just from the things you say about it.

On another note:

Have you ever considered what kind of person you really are? How you look, Sound, Act, Speak, and Think around people? Or just how you behavior in general everywhere you are?

So, let's do a self-analysis – shall we? Are you someone that participate in the things that goes-on around you each day?

Do you speak to people easily? And are you a friendly type of person?

Do people naturally draw to you when you come around?

Do you cause people to feel attached to you from your magnetism?

Are you a person who communicate with others very easily?

Does financial opportunities come to you, naturally?

Are you good at handling pressure, no matter where it comes from?

Can you meet the needs and fulfillments of those who care about you?

Are you someone with an opened mind?

Are you someone who's well-poised, with great magnetism; an electrifying personality that's irresistible, especially with the opposite sex?

**Ask, Questions...**

Asking questions is a sure way to creating new relationships...Here's why:

Questions are, and always will be a successful tool for making friends, or whatever.

When you ask questions, you are naturally opening the world to the unknown for greater opportunities. Any hidden door in life will automatically swing open when you ask the right question. People just don't realize this fact, that's why they go about their lives guessing and assuming things all day long.

Asking questions work, even if nothing else does! And how can anyone resist answering a question; especially if the question is related to directing them toward enriching and enhancing their lifestyle, or drawing the best out of them?                    66

Also, when you ask someone a question, you naturally attract that person to you without them realizing you are doing it to them. So, if you want to have an ice-breaker to getting to know someone; just ask them a question concerning their lifestyle and they will immediately respond to you, because you cause them to start searching inwardly. It's like watching them making a personal discovery right in front of you. It's also how you make great discoveries in your own life as well.

Most people don't know, that, by having questions and expressing them, you can cause anyone to respond to you. And it depends on how, when, and why you ask the question.

You might not want to hear this (if this is the case); but it's true!

– Without having questions; people don't feel alive around you. And they're not curious enough to know more about you. They see you being clueless with nothing in general to talk about. Your conversations aren't interesting. – So they see no reason to know you.

Here's something else to think about …

Every time you ask someone a question, you tap into their curiosity and that cause them to react. They respond without realizing your question makes them open-up to you. – And that's how you become irresistible to people! Questions are a very powerful way to draw people's attention to you.

You see, everyone has questions and answers they want to share. (This is a fact!), because you feel the same way too. – And doesn't it make sense knowing everyone has questions they want answers to?

Just take a closer look at people when you are around them, you see them in a position searching for answers. – You can see this taking place everywhere you are.

Questions are your success formula to all accomplishments you make. And when you know what questions people have, work toward getting the answers to them.

Questions, heats up the mind and heart, making you feel more active and driven.

Here's an exercise you can do, just for the fun of it, with guaranteed results.

– Ask a few people every day, to ask you a question. Once you do this, you will have a courage not too many people have. – Answer every question within reason no matter what it is. – The reason for doing this is getting to know yourself better through the eyes of other people. (Start with those closest to you) to make this easy the way it should be. Then branch-out to other people. – You'll feel it becoming easier once you start doing it.

– For one, you're improving your communication skill with people.

Two, you're discovering what people think, seeing what's goes on inside their mind. Truthfully, you are seeing how people see you. And your questions will teach you how to draw anyone you want to you.

And three, you are basically helping others open-up to better communications with you.

Questions describe who you are, instead of making you defensive to others. Because while you're asking questions you're describing yourself and there's no reason to defend yourself to anyone else, ever again.

With this book, you'll stop going-around in-circle, standing-still in that lifestyle you once lived; because now, that artificial lifestyle doesn't exist any longer, unless you recreate it! And since you have made it this far; you should really feel this down-pour of wisdom and understanding inside you now, because "brighter-visions" are turned-on inside your comprehension toward better living conditions for yourself, and others.

You feel yourself {{Growing}} inside now.

By continuously applying these visions to your life everyday, you will climb to greater heights of accomplishments to whatever you want out of life. And this begin from where you are right now. So keep these visions alive inside you and live a much happier and enriching lifestyle.

From now on, you will see yourself differently, because you are changing the way you look at things, (yourself) for one.

Now let's take a look at those Great Qualities you have inside you:

What would you say; One of, or some of your greatest qualities are today?

During this part of the book, you'll discover what really makes you tick, and how you are naturally affecting people and drawing them closer to you everywhere you are.

For example: The author would say some of his greatest qualities are bringing out the best in people. Public speaking, loving others, writing, teaching, and things like that.

Now it's your turn! – What are some of your greatest qualities?

Stop and think for a few minutes on "One or more" of your greatest qualities. See that part of you that sticks-out the most, because your qualities determines the way you communicate with people – also causes them to be interested, or not interested in you.

As said before, don't just be seen or heard – be felt by others. Allow your Vibes to flow from you naturally. Open yourself up to a whole new experience.

You see, each of us want real answers to our life to live a more fulfilling lifestyle, (the answers are already embedded deep within us) and we have to start somewhere in order to meet those requirements for successful living.

Just remember the three-Big E's...

You are Experimenting with your Experiences fulfilling your Expectations.

One last thing to share:

If you are living by-yourself, eating alone, sleeping alone, or talking to yourself; Why are you doing that? With 7-billion people on this planet, why go at life alone?

And remember: "What One person won't do, Many other people will." – And that's a fact!

Before ending this book, the author want to share something very important with you.

One thing you have to realize, is this; you have freedom of choice embedded deeply inside you. – You cannot sell it. – No one can take it away from you. – Nor can you give it away. – And that's why you are where you are today. You've chosen it this way!

Read this book repeatedly until you feel your comprehensions naturally changing the way you look at thing, so the things you look at around you will start naturally changing for you.

Keep it all simple – everything!

This brings this book to a conclusion.

And remember, this book is written to change our world.

So don't complain about anything else in the world anymore; do something productive to help change it; (Starting with you.)

So thanks for allowing the author to share his love and views for all of humankind as one evolving community.

Author: Wendell L. Hines Sr.

www.ingramcontent.com/pod-product-compliance
Lightning Source LLC
Chambersburg PA
CBHW032029090426
42741CB00006B/787